FIFTY MILES

Also by Sheryl St. Germain

The Small Door of Your Death. Autumn House Press, March 2018.

Words Without Walls: Writers on Addiction, Violence, and Incarceration.
Editor, with Sarah Shotland, Trinity University Press, 2015.

Navigating Disaster: Sixteen Essays of Love and a Poem of Despair.
Louisiana Literature Press, 2012.

Between Song and Story: Essays for the Twenty-first Century.
Editor, with Margaret Whitford, Autumn House Press, 2011.

Let it be a Dark Roux: New and Selected Poems. Autumn House Press, 2007.

Swamp Songs: The Making of an Unruly Woman. University of Utah Press, 2003.

The Journals of Scheherazade. University of North Texas Press, 1996.

How Heavy the Breath of God. University of North Texas Press, 1994.

Je Suis Cadien. Translations of poems of Jean Arceneaux. Cross Cultural, 1994 (chapbook).

Making Bread at Midnight. Slough Press, 1992.

Going Home. Perivale Press, 1989 (chapbook).

The Mask of Medusa. Cross Cultural Communications, 1987 (chapbook).

Sheryl St. Germain's *Fifty Miles* is an honest, whole-hearted exploration of addiction and its aftermath, a study of grief, hope, survival, and the cruel reality of failure. While St. Germain's son Gray did not live to tell his own story, she manages here to tell it with care, compassion, and profound insight. Beautifully-written, deeply-felt, *Fifty Miles* is the story of so many of us who've fought addiction or suffered alongside loved ones caught in the net.

— Dinty W. Moore, *Between Panic & Desire*

These heart-breaking, candid and beautifully crafted essays reach beyond the death of a child. They examine the difficult work of surviving the aftermath. What St. Germain offers is not just her story, but the broader wisdom of distilling grief's many voices. In so doing, she remains an artist of the highest order.

— Barbara Hurd, *Tidal Rhythms* and *Listening to the Savage*

In the era of photoshop and Facebook, we're never been more in need of an honest and vulnerable writer like Sheryl St. Germain. With a poet's ear, a critic's insight, and a mother's fierceness, she investigates the life of her troubled son and her efforts to heal after his death. This is a necessary book for anyone who hopes to understand addiction, grief, healing, or the human heart.

— Beth Ann Fennelly, Poet Laureate of Mississippi,
author of *Heating & Cooling: 52 Micro-Memoirs*

This isn't a book about failed relationships, or loss, or grief, or addiction, or parenting. It is much more than that. To give it a label is to strip away the beauty of it—how these essays dissect and interweave and meditate on the emotional complexities of being part of a world that constantly breaks our hearts. It is about love, yes, and guilt, yes, and pain, yes, and memory that clings and holds and haunts. Sheryl St. Germain has created worlds within these pages—some in the unreal plains of a video game, some in the fraught vulnerabilities of motherhood—where she unspools a life cut short and how to reconcile and forgive and remember.

— Ira Sukrungruang, *Buddha's Dog & other Meditations*

A book to break your heart, then mend it again. In *50 Miles*, poet and memoirist Sheryl St. Germain narrates in finely-wrought essays a story of a multi-generational family beset by problems with addiction that, far too often, proved fatal. Empathetic and brave in her reporting, St. Germain recounts a delicate daisy-chain story of sobriety and survival. Whether trekking in Alaska, hiking in Wyoming, studying glaciers and swamps, or traversing the Amazon, this author seeks understanding. She is the one who crochets the world back together in interlocking loops of yarn and enters gaming environments as a night elf healer avatar to aid fallen warriors—all intentional acts that suggest ways to cultivate healing and resilience. In *50 Miles*, Sheryl St. Germain illuminates a phosphorescent pathway out of the dark cave of devastation and grief, back into sunlight.

— Debra Marquart, *The Horizontal World:
Growing Up Wild in the Middle of Nowhere*

FIFTY MILES

Sheryl St. Germain

Etruscan Press

Etruscan Press
Wilkes University
84 West South Street
Wilkes-Barre, PA 18766
(570) 408-4546

 **Wilkes University**

www.etruscanpress.org

Published 2020 by Etruscan Press
Printed in the United States of America
Cover image: *Surrounded By Hours* (detail) © Bill Gingles, Acrylic on canvas, 40"x30"
Cover design by Carey Schwartzburt
Interior design and typesetting by Todd Espenshade
The text of this book is set in Baskerville.

First Edition

17 18 19 20 5 4 3 2 1

Library of Congress Cataloguing-in-Publication Data

Names: St. Germain, Sheryl, author.
Title: Fifty miles / Sheryl St. Germain.
Description: Wilkes-Barre, PA: Etruscan Press, 2020.
Identifiers: LCCN 2018017729 | ISBN 9780999753446 (46)
Subjects: LCSH: St. Germain, Sheryl--Family. | Mothers and sons-- United States--Biography. | Parents of drug addicts--United States-- Biography. | Drug addicts--Death--Biography. | Women poets, American--Alcohol use. | Women alcoholics--United States--Biography. | Women alcoholics--Rehabilitation--United States--Biography.
Classification: LCC PS3569.T1223 Z46 2020 | DDC 818/.5403--dc23
LC record available at https://lccn.loc.gov/2018017729

Please turn to the back of this book for a list of the sustaining funders of Etruscan Press.

This book is printed on recycled, acid-free paper.

For my father, brothers and son:
Jules St. Germain, Jay St. Germain, André St. Germain, and Gray St. Germain Gideon.
And for all those who have wrestled with addiction.

Whatever
Guides you back
To the world.
That dark so deep
The tiniest light
Will do.

— Gregory Orr

Fifty Miles

FIFTY MILES

Introduction

Most people who compulsively seek to escape through drugs do so because they find their consciousness unbearable. That's the real source of addiction.
— Maia Szalavitz

My son was born into a family cursed with substance abuse. I use the words *addict* and *alcoholic* often in this collection, but it's not without awareness that those words often color too deeply how we see someone. If I say my son and I come from a family of alcoholics and addicts I must also say that we come from a family of workers: carpenters and builders, waitresses, warriors and mechanics, gardeners. We come from a family of politicians and jocks, musicians, book-lovers, drug dealers and dreamers. We come from a family of good cooks and risk-takers, a southern family as proud of its southern roots as it is of its dark handsomeness. But the thing that ties most of us together is a propensity for drink and drugs.

I was raised in New Orleans, a city known for its excesses, a city I left at 27, moving to Dallas with my son's dad before he was born, hoping to escape the fate of others in my family: an alcoholic father dead at 59 of cirrhosis, a brother dead at 23 of a drug overdose, another brother at 41; an aunt dead of overdose at the same age; a nephew dead in his twenties from risk-taking behavior; grandfathers and grandmothers, and great grandfathers and great grandmothers who lived shortened lives, some developing cirrhosis in the throes of alcoholism. A brother-in-law addicted to crack, stabbed to death during a drug deal gone bad. Other relatives are still active substance abusers.

It didn't help to move. Gray, my only son, born in 1984 in Dallas, died thirty years later, in 2014, of a heroin overdose. He'd struggled for many years with alcohol and drug abuse. I wrestled myself with both drugs and alcohol, though alcohol was the hardest of the two to give up. My last drink was in January of 2010. Although I used drugs in my youth, mostly marijuana, LSD, miscellaneous pills when I could get them, and cocaine, culminating with spending part of a year shooting up cocaine, I, like most, walked away from it. I do not know exactly *why* I walked away from it, though, given the family predilection, but the experience of shooting up dope has given me great compassion for those who do not walk away. My greater problem was alcohol, which I used for many years to become someone I could not be without it; three essays in this collection, "To Drink a Glacier," "Call of the Bagpipes," and "The Third Step," illuminate my continuing struggle with alcohol.

No one needs to tell me that genes have complex roles in addiction. I can see it with my own eyes and feel it in my own body. The question I ask myself every day, though, is how did I manage to survive, and my son not. The title essay of this collection, "Fifty Miles," examines that question, though the reader will find no hard-and-fast answers in that essay nor in any of the other essays.

So why read these essays if I offer no answers, when our culture clearly seems to need them?

It's hard to imagine anyone living in the United States who doesn't know of, or has not been affected by, the current epidemic of opioid overdose deaths. A surfeit of numbers and statistics have been offered to bring the crisis home to the general population: 142 Americans die every day of drug overdoses; more people die of overdoses than die in traffic accidents; overdoses are the leading cause of death for those under 50 in the United States; heroin overdoses tripled from 2010-2015; drug overdoses claimed the lives of 72,000 Americans in 2017, a 10% increase from the previous year. The White House panel charged with examining the opioid epidemic asked the President in 2017 to declare a national public health emergency, stating that "America is enduring a death toll equal to September 11th every three weeks."

Statistics and documentary reportage are helpful, but they are not enough, as William Carlos Williams reminds us in this well-known excerpt from "Asphodel, That Greeny Flower:"

> It is difficult
> to get the news from poems
> yet men die miserably every day

for lack
of what is found there.

While I respect the work of statisticians and journalists, and have often relied on their work in my own research, it's my belief that the current opioid crisis is part of a larger spiritual crisis. I understand addiction as a kind of cancer of the spirit, and keep in mind Carl Jung's observation that alcoholism (and, I would add, addiction) is at least partially caused by a spiritual thirst. The "merely rational" will never fully address problems of desire for Spirit that one sees in the alcoholic or addict. This is one reason why, for me, lyric essays, poetry, and literature speak more fully to the thing that stole my son, brothers, and father, than statistics and journalism. To heal from those kinds of losses, we need stories and poetry. As a writer, a recovering alcoholic, and a grieving mother, I need lyricism to feed my own spiritual need.

Many books and articles have been published in the last few years focusing on addiction, and offering solutions based in science, including, most notably, Gabor Maté's flawed but compelling *In the Realm of Hungry Ghosts: Close Encounters with Addiction*, and Maia Szalavitz's insightful *Unbroken Brain*, both of which challenge traditional notions of addiction and treatment. One of my hobbies, as sad as it may seem, has become to read memoirs about addiction and recovery. Enough of these memoirs have been published in recent years to fill several book shelves, including my own favorite, Michael Clune's lyric memoir of his addiction, *White Out: The Secret Life of Heroin*, although I also admire David Carr's more narrative *Night of the Gun*. Perhaps the memoir that comes closest to my own project is David Sheff's *Beautiful Boy: A Father's Journey Through His Son's Addiction*, for obvious reasons, although Sheff's story is structured, unlike mine, more as a cohesive narrative. His choice to privilege narrative makes sense, since he comes from a journalistic background, while my background is poetry, thus my bias towards lyricism. Sheff's son, Nic, survived to write his own two memoirs of addiction, *Tweak*, and *We All Fall Down*.

My story is not like any of these memoirs, however, in that my son did not live. He could not write his own memoir because he did not survive to write it. I could not write about his road to recovery because he did not, in the end, recover. We like happy endings in America, and the ending of my son's story is not happy, because he dies, although I live, and this collection is also very much a story of my own survival and healing.

Gray was diagnosed with ADD when he was very small, and wound up taking Ritalin and later Adderall for most of his life, which were the drugs he first abused as a teenager. When he was around nineteen I completed and tried—half-heartedly, it must be said—to publish a memoir about raising a son with ADD. The few publishers and agents I sent it to were uninterested mostly because there was no happy ending, although I would argue I held out hope in the end. The drugs prescribed to help with his ADD had helped a little in the short run, but eventually Gray experienced all the severe problems we had been told he'd experience if we didn't give him the drugs. I thought it important to show the dark side of the stimulants we give ADD-diagnosed children, especially those children who come from a family with a history of substance abuse. I soon gave up trying to publish the manuscript because just a few months after I finished it all hell broke loose. I had to have Gray committed for drug and alcohol abuse, he was diagnosed with bipolar disorder as well as drug use disorder, and everything else in my life fell to the side. The essay "Do No Harm," is excerpted from that unpublished manuscript. In this essay, I highlight the role of schools and our cultural bias toward drugging young children.

This collection, like that unpublished manuscript, does not have a happy ending, if by that we mean survival of its main character, my son. But this is a book about hope. Many of the pieces here are about the ways I stayed sane, or tried to, while Gray was creating and living in ever darker worlds, and then how I worked with grief after he died, specifically through traditional arts such as crochet, and through travelling, gaming, teaching, and writing.

I learned to crochet at my mother's lap as a child, and have worked with yarn most of my life. "It's Come Undone: Crocheting and Catastrophe" traces the ways in which I used the craft of crochet to find peace and a sense of usefulness when things seemed hopeless.

I've always taken succor from the natural world. My first poems were celebrations of that broken world of polluted lakes, crawfish-filled ditches, wondrous blackberries that pricked fingers but tasted like summer sun, and the seductive Mississippi that surrounded me as a girl growing up in Louisiana. I tried to share this love of nature with Gray, and some of the essays mention the camping trips we took when he was young. Later when I had the opportunity to take him to Europe, I did, thinking perhaps to broaden his horizons, hoping that a new landscape would jolt him awake, as it often did me.

After he died I continued to travel, often to the Netherlands, as my second husband is Dutch, and to France, where a beloved artist's retreat in the Languedoc area, La Muse, had provided solace and inspiration in the past. Pieces collected here are also inspired by visits to Peru with students, as well as Florida and Wyoming, where I went for artist retreats. Grief does not remain home when you travel, but being in different landscapes allows new lenses on that grief. The cycle of life and death is ever on vibrant display in the natural world. If you're lucky, walks and hikes in the natural world can offer ways to understand your changed world, insights, and encouragement to continue living.

The longest piece in the collection, "Parking Lot Nights," an essay inspired by video games, is also partly about travelling, as I would argue that playing certain kinds of games, especially role-playing games, can function as a kind of travel. I've been a gamer much of my adult life, thanks to my son, and this essay traces my relationship with Gray through gaming, and offers some discussion about the ways in which video games might offer metaphors through which we can connect with each other in surprisingly profound ways. The essay also looks at the ways in which gaming helped me both grieve and heal.

Writing is a key tool in healing, and a couple of pieces address that explicitly: "Essay in Search of a Poem," for example, which traces my attempts to write a poem too soon after Gray's death. Underlying all these pieces, though, even the ones not explicitly about writing, is the need to find a writing structure that houses grief honestly, especially in the second section, which was written in the aftermath of Gray's death. The pieces in the second section are, for the most part, shorter, because they were written closer to the death, when any attempt at narrative seemed like a lie. The early pieces in this section, especially the first really short ones like "First Days" and "The Amaryllis Bud," function more like fragments, prose poems, if you will. Anyone who has experienced tragedy knows that all one can do for a time is wail, and it seemed important to acknowledge that.

Many of the travel pieces are also in this section, and eventually the reader can witness me able to reflect more calmly, riffing off new landscapes to explore the landscape of grief inside.

The final piece of the second section, "Memory, Ever Green," written in Paris, is built around memories of my father's life, and asks questions about how we might best remember those we love who have destroyed their lives with drink or other substances.

The decision to make this book a collection of essays rather than one unbroken narrative was one I thought about for a long time. Wouldn't there be a larger audience for an uninterrupted narrative, one that moved inevitably through beginning, conflict, resolution, the traditional art of story? Maybe, but to camouflage the way in which grief and healing moves in fits and starts, as well as the fits and starts of a life caught in addiction seemed to me the most profound of falsehoods. Some of the pieces in this collection were written before Gray died, and I did not want to go back and change them to reflect my knowledge that he would soon die. It felt more honest to let them stand as genuine moments in time.

It also seemed wrong to try to make all the pieces seem as if they were written in one voice. Depending on what the essay seems to need I might write in first, second or third person. Sometimes the essays are excruciatingly personal and other times I use a more distanced approach. There's at least one poem in the collection, depending on how you define poetry. I haven't tried to project a single voice or a single narrative, as we don't all speak and think with one voice. Sometimes I'm an angry mother, sometimes a grieving one. Sometimes I write as a poet, sometimes as an essayist. Sometimes I privilege lyricism, sometimes narrative. Sometimes I write as a teacher, sometimes a critic. I am always writing as an alcoholic. I am all of these things, just as my son was a musician, a passionate lover of science fiction and video games, an angry young man, a depressed young man, a loving young man, an alcoholic, and an addict.

Although AA was important for me in the early days of my own recovery, and though I still cherish the friends and community I found there, I couldn't complete all the steps (see "The Third Step" for one take on why), so I took what seemed useful and left the rest. One of the things I did take from AA, however, was the message of Step 12: "Having had a spiritual awakening as the result of these Steps, we tried to carry this message to alcoholics, and to practice these principles in all our affairs." Having personally experienced the ways in which writing could encourage healing and assist with recovery, in 2007 I co-founded, with Sarah Shotland, Words Without Walls, a program that sends MFA students and faculty into jails, prisons, and rehabilitation facilities to teach creative writing. I teach myself as part of the program in Sojourner House, an in-house rehab center for women who are mothers. "The Ink That Binds: Creative Writing and Addiction," the final essay in the collection, was inspired by teaching in this facility.

My son once said to me that he didn't think he could be creative (and by that he meant write music) without being high. This made me sad because I know a great number of writers (including myself) who are in recovery and still able to be creative. Facilitating a group that supported each other in creative fellowship, a group that could then go on to share with others, seemed a good way to "pass it on."

This collection tells two stories, one of a fall, and one of healing, and is yet another way, I hope, of passing it on.

I

Do No Harm

The week before my son started kindergarten, I trimmed the long hair tail I'd let him grow. He hadn't wanted me to trim it because, he said, if it got long enough, he'd become a lady, which seemed sort of cool to him at the time. It was 1989, and we were living in Dallas, Texas. A photograph taken on his first day of school shows him wearing a new Batman sweatshirt, stonewashed jeans, and new sneakers. He's standing in front of his new school, Lakewood Elementary, holding a purple lunch box and smiling brightly. His blonde hair, tail-less, is neatly combed to the side. It's one of the saddest photographs I own. He's happy, naïve, full of promise, and his future seems as unmarred as the cloudless August morning. I was excited that first day too. All the hustle and bustle, all the children in their new clothes, all the hopeful faces of the parents mirroring my own. The new cars and well-dressed moms and dads dropping off their well-dressed kids impressed me. For the last three years, I'd been divorced from Gray's father, putting myself through graduate school, and Gray and I had been living just above the poverty line. Now I had a part-time teaching job and two roommates to help with the rent. For the first time since we'd left his father, Gray and I were living in a "good" neighborhood.

He came home from school that first week quiet; I couldn't get him to talk much about how things were going. On Friday morning, though, when I woke him, he rubbed his eyes and said, "Today is tomorrow, Mommy."

"What do you mean, sweetie? Today is today. It's Friday, a school day."

"No, it's Saturday. I don't have to go to school today," he said, pulling the covers over his head.

After some cajoling and threatening, I got him out of bed and to school on time, but since I'm an educator myself, I was disappointed that he seemed already disenchanted with school. That night, he had a series of nightmares, one about a two-foot long scorpion, another about a kidnapper who could take his head off and put it back on, and the last involving his teacher, who appeared as a witch with a magic diamond that made kids look ugly. He slept with me that night.

Monday afternoon, one week into the term, I discovered a note from the principal in Gray's book bag. At the top was the Dallas Independent School District letterhead. Below, the principal had handwritten:

Parents of Gray Gideon:
Please see me as soon as possible about several problems that Gray is having at school. His teacher is having problems with him, and I have had to correct Gray many times during and after lunch.
Larry Williams, Principal

After dropping Gray off the next morning, I met with the principal in his office. He was a short, plump man, balding and ruddy-cheeked, who spoke with a heavy Texas accent. He looked me square in the face.

"I'll get right to the point, Mrs. Gideon. Your son has Attention Deficit Disorder. He needs to be put on Ritalin."

To say I was stunned at the abruptness of his pronouncement would be an understatement.

"It's St. Germain, not Gideon," I said. "And you know this after *one week* with my son?"

He gave me a patronizing look and proceeded to explain. He noted not only Gray's fidgetiness and inability to sit still, but that he had trouble getting started on projects and trouble finishing them. He seemed to be "out in space" somewhere when the teacher gave orders or assignments. He couldn't remember much of anything, his teacher Mrs. Merkin had said. Whenever he had to go somewhere, whether it was to the bathroom or outside for recess, he ran. Sometimes, the principal said, he even ran in the classroom from one side to the other. These, he said, were symptoms of ADD[1] children—restlessness, hyper-activity, inability to concentrate for long periods of time, and so on. He told me he had written his dissertation on ADD, which was why he could recognize it so quickly. ADD children, if not treated, he said, tended to fall behind and become under-achievers. Some of them, he said, never finished school and had trouble making friends all of their lives.

"Mrs. Merkin has had to send Gray in here to talk with me every day because he won't sit still and can't pay attention. He's distracting the other students and interfering with their ability to learn."

"Every day?"

"Every day. And this can't go on."

"But this is just kindergarten. It's the first time he's *had* to sit still. Why can't the teacher handle this herself?"

"Kindergarten is an important time for children, Mrs. Gideon. It prepares them for the challenges ahead. The teacher can't take so much time on one child. It's better to nip this in the bud now."

I left his office furious. Of course I knew about ADD (Attention Deficit Disorder); I'd read articles in the newspapers and magazines about how it was being over-diagnosed in young children, mostly boys, and how Ritalin was a stimulant often used treat it. ADD was associated with hyperactivity, but its major symptoms were inattention and impulsivity. Tears sprung, unbidden. I didn't want to drug Gray. The thought of it made me ill, but I wondered what would happen if we fought the principal's recommendation. I felt thrust into a harsh world I didn't understand, and for the first time in my life, I had no clue what the right path might be. It seemed to me that, once taken, the path of drugs would be one from which it would be hard to turn back.

Psychostimulants were first administered to children in 1937, although the first FDA-approved use of Ritalin (methylphenidate) for children was in 1961. Methylphenidate, classified in the same category as cocaine and methamphetamine, is a stimulant some doctors argue is ad-

---

[1] Though this diagnosis is now referred to as ADHD (Attention Deficit Hyperactivity Disorder), I use ADD in this essay because that was the term used when Gray was diagnosed in the late eighties, early nineties.

dicting. For years, it has been abused on the streets, sometimes crushed and snorted, other times injected. Like cocaine, it's a powerful, mind-altering drug. During the 1990's, the use of Ritalin or other stimulants to control children's behavior increased more than seven hundred percent in the United States. Data from the Centers for Disease Control and Prevention show that the number of children on medication for ADD has risen from 600,000 in 1990 to 3.5 million in 2014.

Retired deputy assistant administrator of the DEA Gene Haislip commented that America has become the only country in the world whose children are prescribed such a vast quantity of stimulants that share the same properties as cocaine. The United States uses about eighty-five percent of the world's Ritalin.

When I thought of Gray, I thought of exuberance, ebullience. His face was always radiant with emotion, and he was literally filled with energy, curiosity and enthusiasm for everything. Tickled by some event or other, he would sometimes throw his body recklessly through the air and onto his bed, ripped through with laughter. He would be unaware of the room, or of me, only attentive to the absurd thing that had made him laugh, and the hole of laughter into which he'd fallen. He was so animated, so full of ideas and questions, and already adamant in his opinions. What would this child be like on Ritalin?

I thought of *Where the Wild Things Are*, the Caldecott Medal-winning book by Maurice Sendak, which I read to Gray probably once a week. Everything about the protagonist, Max, the child in wolf's clothing—his truculent and defiant nature, his "wildness," his imagination, his restless body and spirit—reminded me of Gray. What kind of culture did I live in, where the same qualities that were admired and celebrated in a book were labeled as a disorder in the schools?

I could feel myself becoming stubborn, digging in against the principal's recommendation, though I had little but intuition to support my yet unshaped feelings. It did seem, however, that drugs should be the last recourse, not the first. The accusation that Gray was inattentive baffled me; he had never been inattentive at home. He loved being read to, and he paid attention even when the books we read were long and didn't have many pictures. He loved playing with his toys, certainly showing great attention there. True, I sometimes had to tell him several times to do something, and he was occasionally defiant, but that seemed to me healthy, a sort of testing of boundaries and limits that needn't be pathologized. I was angry, though I couldn't say at whom or what.

The way Ritalin was explained to parents in those days was a little like the way God is explained to young children: it's a mystery in which you must have faith. Ritalin, doctors told us, was a stimulant that, on children, had the opposite effect. It somehow calmed them down instead of speeding them up. I could not wrap my head around the paradox that a stimulant could act as a sedative. We now know that Ritalin does not have a paradoxical effect on children; it affects them exactly as it affects adults, as a stimulant. Like methadone, it provides a substitute "high"; the stimulation is drug-produced so that kids don't search for stimulation in the real world. According to Lawrence Diller, author of *Running on Ritalin*, what observers mistake for calm is intensified focus.

We weren't doing our jobs as parents, the principal said, if we didn't put Gray on Ritalin. In subsequent conversations, the principal continually emphasized that the consequences of not putting Gray on Ritalin were school failure such that he would eventually drop out, depression, conduct disorder, failed relationships, underachievement in the workplace, and substance abuse.

I decided, however, to resist the principal's suggestion that we put Gray on Ritalin. I came from a family that had a history of substance abuse, and I did not wish to set my son on the road to drug use as a way to control his behavior. I had escaped the fate of many in my family, and would do everything in my power to help my son escape. Sanctioned or not, Ritalin had the same effects as cocaine, effects I knew well.

Before I left the principal's office, I informed him I'd consider what he had said, but that either way I was going to sit in on Gray's class. I also called Gray's father and explained to him what the principal had said. We had a long conversation in which we agreed to try to make the environments at each house more similar, to have the same rules, the same consequences for breaking the rules, and make sure he was eating balanced meals at regular intervals at both homes. Consistency, we decided, was key.

I attended Gray's kindergarten class the following Tuesday. I wanted Mrs. Merkin to forget I was there, so I brought some papers to grade, and since I myself didn't teach on Tuesdays, I settled in for the whole day.

Mrs. Merkin was in her mid-twenties and could not have been teaching for very long. The class was large, with almost thirty students, and she clearly did not have the skills to manage such a crowded class. During the morning period, she constantly sent children—always boys—to the principal's office, sometimes for minor infractions. Gray did not get into trouble that day (he was acutely aware that I was there), but I watched with interest as one little boy who, during a long period of coloring, decided to finish coloring standing up, was dressed down by Mrs. Merkin. She insisted he sit down to finish the coloring. Each time she turned around, he stood up again, still coloring, but standing and bending over the table. She'd run back to the table, order him to sit down, and the cycle would repeat. By the end of it, she was shrieking, the boy was sobbing, and she had grabbed him roughly by his collar and dragged him out the door and into the principal's office. I was flabbergasted. If she acted this way while a parent was watching, I wondered what went on with no parent present.

Anything Mrs. Merkin taught, she taught by rote. There was no spark, no enthusiasm in her. She read the most mundane, simplistic stories to the kids in a monotonous, singsong voice. I read to Gray every night: *The Odyssey, Watership Down, The Hobbit*. He already knew most of his letters and could recognize many words. *She* was boring, the class was boring, and I didn't blame Gray for acting out. Not only that, but she was inflexibly authoritarian, and I could see why Gray might buck against her rigid rules. Students had to sit utterly still almost every moment they were in the classroom, and then they had to lie still for forty-five minutes of "quiet time," during which they couldn't even look at picture books. Students were not allowed to talk during lunch either. I found this last an unbelievably harsh rule, but she defended it by saying that if they allowed the students to talk, they wouldn't finish their meals on time. And who knows what unholy chaos would break out if they didn't finish their meals on time?

If, as some contemporary researchers have suggested, ADD-diagnosed kids are addicted to sensory stimulation, being unable to engage with each other during lunchtime and then being forced to lie down for forty-five minutes with no stimulation must be torturous. Even if one doesn't buy the theory that they are addicted to sensory stimulation, it's unreasonable to expect that five-year-olds might willingly sit still during the whole of class with one recess break of fifteen minutes, have lunch where they can't socialize, and be forced to lie still or take a forced nap for another forty-five minutes. It occurred to me after just one day in Gray's class that not only does the traditional public-school structure privilege docile, obedient personalities, but for some children it constitutes a very real form of torture, all the worse because it's sanctioned by those who most care about the children.

Later that evening, I asked Gray what he thought of Mrs. Merkin.

"She's stupid!"

I didn't say anything, although I actually agreed with him.

"She doesn't even know how to pronounce some things. And she keeps calling me *Greg*."

After a week of sitting in Mrs. Merkin's class, I demanded that Gray be switched to another teacher. The principal said they didn't usually switch teachers, but I was adamant, and eventually he gave in. Gray was put into a more seasoned teacher's class, Mrs. Snyder's class. I sat in the first day of class with her, too, and could see she was a bit more effective than Mrs. Merkin. She didn't constantly send kids to the principal's office but rather tried to handle infractions herself.

Things were okay for a little while, then Gray started to get in trouble again – notes were being sent home about him being fidgety and not paying attention. I began speaking with Mrs. Snyder several times a week, but nothing either of us did helped. Soon I got another call from the principal to meet with him.

The night before we were to meet, I read Gray another chapter of *The Hobbit* and snuggled in bed next to him. He was holding one of the stuffed animals he'd had since birth, the one we called "heart bear" because a red heart was stitched to its chest. I stroked his hair.

"How are you liking school these days?" I asked.

He looked at me with his startling gray eyes, which began to fill with tears. Then he looked at his bear, and when he spoke, it seemed as if he were speaking to the bear, not me.

"I wish there was a world where principals didn't beat children," he said.

It turned out that during many of those visits to the principal's office, the principal had been beating Gray with a paddle he kept in his desk drawer. I learned, to my surprise, that corporal punishment was legal in Texas. School officials did not need the approval of the parent to hit a child, nor did they have to inform the parents. Furious, frustrated, and emotionally bereft, I reminded myself we were in the middle of the Bible Belt, where many believed that to spare the rod was to spoil the child, but that didn't help much. The week before, the *Dallas Morning News* had published an article about the use of corporal punishment in schools. The principal of a Texas Christian elementary school had been quoted as saying, "We should be passing bills to *encourage* corporal punishment."

The next morning, I marched into the principal's office determined to let him have it. He motioned me to sit down and pulled the paddle out of his drawer. Years later, Gray would say to me, "Do you remember that principal who beat me? Did you know his paddle had pictures of the Smurfs on it? Isn't that sick?"

In that moment, I didn't notice the images on the paddle. As the principal stroked it, I only registered that it was painted bright enamel blue and peppered with brightly colored stickers.

"You have to understand, Mrs. Gideon, that if you refuse to have Gray tested for ADD, we have to take other measures." He paused. "You know, one problem with Gray is that he's not afraid."

"What do you mean he's not afraid?"

"He's not afraid. He comes in here, knowing he's going to be paddled, and he stands there, defiant, and refuses to apologize or promise that he won't misbehave." The principal tapped the paddle against the palm of his hand, thinking.

"He's only five years old!"

"Why do you think he's not afraid, Mrs. Gideon?"

"St. Germain, Sheryl St. Germain, I don't have Gray's dad's last name. Please don't call me that again. And I guess he's not afraid because he's never *had* to be afraid."

"Don't you discipline him at home?"

"He has to do quiet time when he does something wrong."

"Does that work?"

"Sometimes it does, sometimes it doesn't."

"What about your husband?"

"What *about* my husband?" I felt like he was speaking a foreign language.

"Does he discipline your son?"

"We both do quiet time. We try to be consistent." Instead of building up to tell the principal off, I was weakening. I could feel myself becoming emotional, and I knew that if I didn't get out of there soon, I was going to cry. I couldn't bear the thought of this man hitting my son, however sanctioned it might be.

"Well," he said, "once you get him on Ritalin, I'm sure he'll be in here less often. It really does help, you know. The teachers like it. It helps them do their job and keep order in the classroom. And Gray will find that he's better able to make friends too. Right now, I don't think too many of his classmates want to hang around him because he's always getting in trouble."

"But this is just kindergarten!" I said. I was beginning to feel like I was in a Kafka novel. Nothing made sense. "I thought kids just colored and hung out and got used to each other in kindergarten. Since when did it become like the army?"

I felt like I was suffocating. I left the principal's office and drove around and around the neighborhood, looking at the homes of the parents and children who went to Gray's school. I had never noticed how neatly clipped and submissive their hedges looked, how their trees were pruned until they looked like spiritless soldiers. I wondered if the children playing in the yards were well-beaten children. I had thought I'd done the right thing trying to move into what was supposed to be a good school district, but now I was confused. *Had* I done the right thing? Why hadn't I told the principal never to touch my son again? What kind of wimp was I? Was I so unsure of my own methods? I had to conclude that I was. What did I know about raising kids? Gray was my only child.

I remembered the beatings my father used to give us. His belt always hung on the back of his easy chair, and if we did anything wrong, we would "get the belt." I remember being whipped so hard my thighs blistered. I don't remember it ever changing anything, but I do remember it making me mad, then humiliated, and then I'd cry and my father would eventually stop. He was usually measured when he meted out punishment to the girls, but my brothers really got it, especially Jay, who was always in trouble, and who wound up dropping out of school, going to prison, and dying in his early twenties of a drug overdose. He got a lot of beatings, and my father would sometimes go into a rage when he beat him. Sometimes he was drunk, my father, and the beatings would last longer, though they'd be sloppier. Jay and Gray shared enough traits—asthma, defiance, trouble with authority, problems attending and organizing—that I was already beginning to worry that Gray might share Jay's fate. Jay would surely have been diagnosed with ADD had he been born a generation later. Would Ritalin have saved him? Repeated beatings surely had not.

I imagined the principal beating Gray. I imagined what Gray must have been feeling. Rivers rising in him, flooding, unchecked, something in him drowning. The principal saying he needs to learn fear. My father beating and beating my brother, throwing him up, down, against the door. For each demerit a beating, my brother not giving in, not hitting back, not crying in front of anyone. Like my son, maybe, the welts rising in his heart, his guts twisting and weeping.

Over the next weeks, I spent several nights sleepless, the principal's words and his twangy Texas accent infecting every conscious moment: *You have to understand that if you refuse to have Gray tested for ADD, we have to take other measures.* So, were these my options? Drug him or beat him? Suddenly, Ritalin didn't seem like such a bad choice.

Corporal punishment is a time-honored and traditional method of discipline in American schools. Historically, it was seen as a method of literally "beating the devil" out of misbehaving children. Learning theorists, however, argue that punishment as a means of behavior control is complex, and that it can accelerate or retard performance of some behavior. A child can habituate to punishment and, if beaten enough, become a psychopath. Every study I could find on corporal punishment suggested it led to violence and aggression rather than self-discipline. It made tragic sense to me that Texas, the state with the worst record for the death penalty, would also be the leading practitioner of corporal punishment in the schools.

In 1999, almost 74,000 of Texas's 3.9 million students were paddled. About eighty-three percent were boys, according to a U.S. Department of Education survey. (Unsurprisingly, the percentage of boys versus
girls diagnosed with ADD is around the same.) In 1989, the year Gray
started kindergarten, Texas was one of very few states that had no proce-
dural requirements for corporal punishment. Teachers needn't have approval of the principal; the punishment did not have to take place in the
presence of another adult, or without undue anger. It did not have to be
reasonable, nor did the punishers have to have approval from the parents.
School officials could strike on the head and face, and there was no re-
striction against deadly force. It could even take place in presence of other
students.

Most researchers agree that corporal punishment often appears to
result in the temporary reduction of undesirable behavior, and in this it is
not unlike Ritalin. To be effective in the long run, however, the punishment
must be extremely harsh and repeated—and even then, the results are
inconclusive. In an essay about the link between corporal punishment and
delinquency, Ralph Welsh writes that no recidivist male delinquent existed
who had never been exposed to corporal punishment, be it a belt, a board,
an extension cord, or a fist.

As late as 1994, almost all the southern states still allowed corporal
punishment in their schools. When George W. Bush ran for president, he
won electoral college votes from nineteen of the twenty-two states that
allow corporal punishment, a figure so stark, some extremists were moved
to call him "the president with the child-beating mandate." Although, to
my knowledge, former President Bush has not spoken out in favor of corporal punishment, his education bill included the Teacher Protection Act,
a provision to protect principals and other school officials from lawsuits
by parents of beaten children. (This provision was removed from the bill
by members of his own party.) As governor of Texas during Gray's childhood, Governor Bush also signed more death warrants than any other
living government official.

Today, thirty-one states have banned corporal punishment. Texas is
among nineteen states where it remains legal, leaving it up to individual school
districts to determine whether students may be struck. In August 2003, under
increasing pressure from its community after information regarding several

injuries students sustained from corporal punishment, the Dallas Independent School District revised its corporal punishment policy, stopping short of prohibiting paddling. School authorities may still paddle, but they must have a written request from the parents that this method of discipline be used.

I met again with Gray's principal and requested that he not paddle Gray. I continued to sit in on his classroom a few times a month, with increasing despair. Even though Mrs. Snyder was a more seasoned teacher, little meaningful one-on-one interaction occurred with students. The classroom was too big for any kind of learning except rote. Students were rushed from one subject to another; never was there a sense of completion or interconnectedness. It was incredibly tedious, and I could see how bright students might come to see school as a boring, essentially meaningless activity. Surely it was not the same at a private school, I began to think, but when Gray's father and I investigated the private schools in Dallas, our hearts sank. There was no way we could afford them.

I remembered my mother wringing her hands in despair at my brother's funeral, crazed with grief, saying over and over, "His kindergarten class was too large, the teacher had a nervous breakdown, he needed more attention . . .." She believed then, and still believes to this day, that my brother's subsequent problems, and his eventual tragic death, could be traced back to that kindergarten class, which had been too large. Psychologists would consider her analysis of the situation utterly simplistic, and yet—if the child's first experience with formal education, which will take up such a large portion of his or her formative years, is unrelentingly negative, it will surely take a tremendous effort on the part of overworked teachers and harried and often untrained parents to change that impression.

When I think of a tiny five-year-old—Gray was always the smallest child in his class, and even now, at twenty-nine, is only five foot six—going up against a heavy-set authoritarian principal with a paddle, an instrument Gray had never seen, I am cut to the core.

Gray must have been shamed by the sessions with the principal, else he would have told me about them earlier. What choices did he have, as a child, in response to these beatings? Accept and acquiesce, or defy and be beaten. He chose the latter as a five-year-old, and it was a choice he would make continually for the next fifteen years in repeated conflicts with authority figures. In my most painful confrontations with Gray in his teen years, however, when I caught his eyes, I always saw the eyes of a spunky five-year-old. They were the eyes of a five-year-old confronting a hulking principal with a paddle, a five-year-old confronting an adult who wants to beat fear into him, a five-year-old confronting a version of his nightmare-witch with the magic diamond that makes kids look ugly.

We managed to squeeze Gray through kindergarten without Ritalin, but promised the school we would consider trying it before he started first grade. Gray's pediatrician also thought it worth trying. "You can always stop it if you don't like what it does to him, Sheryl. It really does help a lot of kids," he said. By this time, Gray was seeing a counselor who also believed in the value of Ritalin.

It was hard to continue to fight the school, the doctors, *and* Gray's dad, who was beginning to lean on me. The principal had threatened to go back to the paddling if Gray's behavior didn't improve, hinting that, legally, he did not need my permission to paddle him.

Gray continued to have problems in school, and needed a lot of support from the teachers, his father, and me to complete school projects. Yet his grades were good. In Pre-reading, Writing, Mathematics, Science, and Art he got straight E's throughout the year. Under "Personal and Social Development," however, he got an *X* (the equivalent of an *F)* in "follows directions," "completes assigned tasks," "works well with others," and "exhibits self-control." He got an *X* in "makes good use of time."

Eventually, I caved. I caved to the pressure from the school, the doctors, and Gray's father, and I agreed to put Gray on Ritalin when he turned seven.

As far as I know, the principal never beat him again.

Gray would remain on Ritalin or some substitute—in later years it was Adderall—for at least twelve years, during which period he continued to have problems with friendships, his grades deteriorated, and he developed more strongly defiant behavior at school. In high school, he was suspended several times for his insolence toward the teachers, and he was arrested a few times for minor offenses. Eventually, he stopped going to classes and had to go to court on several occasions for truancy. He dropped out of high school at sixteen, still taking psycho-stimulants. Although he managed to get a GED and make it through half a semester of college with Adderall, he began to abuse that drug, as many do, and I wound up having to commit him for drug abuse when he was nineteen. In later years, he would convince doctors to give him other versions of stimulants such as Concerta, Focalin, and Vyvanse. He would graduate to meth and even heroin. At this writing, he has just completed thirty days of rehab.

I don't know how much effect the years of taking stimulants will ultimately have on Gray's life. It was moderately useful in the early years, ineffective in the teen years, and overall, does not appear to have had the promised positive effects. I sometimes fear that his natural impulsivity, creativity, and spontaneity were squelched during those years he was on stimulants, and maybe those years of squelching contributed to the strong feelings in him that are sometimes manifested as anger. It's as if the drug managed to hold back those waters for a time, but now all the floodgates are open, and all hell has burst loose.

All the things the principal and ADD literature claimed would be the consequences of not putting Gray on Ritalin—school failure such that he would eventually drop out, depression, conduct disorder, failed relationships, under-achievement in the workplace, and substance abuse—have occurred anyway, despite the use of stimulants. I asked him recently about his use of drugs and alcohol to control his moods, and he said that he learned as a child that the way the culture wanted him to control his moods was with a pill, so he never learned to develop the life skills he needed to manage his emotions.

Gray still struggles with the same issues he struggled with in kindergarten. And yet. My son is one of the smartest persons I have ever known. He has more natural intelligence than many of my PhD-educated colleagues. He is a talented musician, poet, and social critic. He is witty and has a great sense of humor. But he is a failure in the eyes of American society.

Life is messy. I've focused exclusively on one thread of that mess here: the negative effects of a broken school system. Of course, other crucial strands, both environmental and cultural, affected Gray's life. Kids like Gray often have behavior problems that have little to do with those behavior clusters psychologists label as ADD. Genes and culture figure into the mix, parenting styles as well as the style of authority and learning in the schools.

Perhaps most importantly, though, schools have failed to understand how radically different this generation is from those that preceded it, and how the popular American culture that bred and nurtured Gray's generation had a tremendous influence on their ability to attend as well as their capacity for defiance.

Gray's generation, often called Millennials, was the first generation to be inundated with a fast-moving popular culture—including video games, MTV, and web surfing—that created and then nurtured a kind of aesthetics of movement. Popular media breastfed these kids on montage, breakneck speed images, and fractured narratives. Most experienced changing landscapes in more personal ways as well, as a large percent of them came from single parent families where partners came and went, and actual physical movement, from house to house if not from state to state, was the norm. This was certainly the case with Gray. I left his father when he was eighteen months old, and we moved every few years after that in search of a better job or neighborhood.

Gray's was the first generation whose defining features, specifically their short attention span, lack of respect for authority, and seeming lack of ambition were pathologized. If we accept that Attention Deficit Disorder is in fact a disorder, Gray's generation was the one to which it was first applied almost wholesale, as was the practice of using stimulants to control it. Our attitude has been to punish or drug the kids, and to demonize rather than try to understand the culture that influences them.

Once a diagnosis of ADD is made of a child, that label tends to dominate how we see that child. No longer do we see a child with a cultural and personal history, a child (and parents) caught in a struggle with a sometimes idiotic school system over which all may feel powerless, a bright, quick, heartbreakingly insightful and imaginative child; we see a child with ADD. The label functions as a pair of sunglasses we put on whenever we look at our child, glasses that mute the brightness, shade the subtle but important colors. In that respect, Gray's nightmare about the magic diamond that makes kids look ugly is quite appropriate.

The most striking common denominators of ADD children are their painful difficulties in our public-school system and the profound failure of the schools to find a way to embrace and nurture these children. The way Gray's school chose to deal with him is typical of what we still find in many American schools: drug or punish. And though there are, as I've noted, many issues, both cultural and genetic, that we need to consider when thinking about these children, it is the issue of schooling over which we have most power, as a culture, to affect. We can't change genes, we can't always change popular culture, we can't always change the way a parent interacts with a child. We can, however, change the way our public schools treat children.

The medical profession has as its motto *do no harm,* and this is the very least we can ask of our school system. Gray has come of age in a world of perhaps unparalleled violence and aggression. Is it surprising that a nation that still allows its children to be beaten in schools produces soldiers who can perform the kinds of physical abuse of international prisoners we have witnessed in the media over the last few years? It can also come as no surprise that, in 2014, one in three students claim to have been bullied at school, and that the rise in other school-related violence, including the recent widely publicized school shootings, has reached an obscene level.

Grays' principal was practicing, on a small scale, the principles of terrorism. Even though the principal believed my son had a disorder that did not allow him to attend, despite his belief that my son needed medication to "behave," he still beat him, just as we still execute death-row prisoners who are demonstrably mentally ill. The principal, by his own admission, wanted to instill terror in my son's heart. It didn't work, although it succeeded in wounding him, possibly, I worry, for the rest of his life.

Friedrich Nietzsche, in *Beyond Good and Evil,* cautions those of us who fight monsters to take care that we not become monsters ourselves. Let's begin by shining our magic diamonds such that we do not see our children as monsters. Let's at least consider that through gross neglect, our schools may have become torture chambers for some of our children. Let's stop relying on drugs and punishment as the major tools in our toolboxes to deal with these children.

Let's do something radical: let's work on understanding generations so wondrously strange and challenging. I am only one mother writing about a son and a generation for whom this advice comes too late. If our unhappy story can change just a few people's minds about what we are doing to our children in our schools, it is worth the pain of having had to tell it.

For the next generations.

Note:

The few studies that exist looking at ADHD-diagnosed children and later addiction are inconclusive; some suggest that children treated with stimulants have a lower rate of addiction to other substances, while others suggest that use of stimulants in childhood can lead to later addiction. In *Dopesick*, her recent book charting the opioid crisis, Beth Macy writes "Almost to a person, the addicted twentysomethings I met had taken attention-deficit medication as children, prescribed pills that as they entered adolescence morphed from study aid to party aid." Macy quotes Dr. Anna Lembke, an addiction medicine specialist at Stanford University School of Medicine: ". . . if we really believe that addiction is a result of changes in the brain due to chronic heavy drug exposure, how can we believe that stimulant exposure isn't going to change these kids' brains in a way that makes them more vulnerable to harder drugs?"[2]

Between 2000 and 2010, diagnosis of children with ADHD rose 25% in the United States. If there is even a small chance of a relationship between early stimulant use in children and later addiction we should be concentrating massive amounts of resources into researching that connection.

---

[2] *Dopesick: Dealers, Doctors, and the Drug Company That Addicted America*, Beth Macy. Little Brown and Company, 2018. pp. 134-135.

Fireflies

When Gray was in junior high we lived in Iowa where he stayed with me in the summers, and with his dad, in Dallas, for the school year. I would feel sad when the fireflies came in August because I knew it was almost time for him to return to his father's. We had a ritual of going out to watch fireflies the evening before he had to leave.

One August evening in those years we took our last walk of the summer to the park near our house. Gray ran around the open field in the park's center, buoyed by an energy my body had long forgotten, sweat shining on his forehead like a kind of body-light in the setting sun. He ran to the merry-go-round and pushed it in faster and faster circles.

"Hey mom, look at this!" he yelled, hanging on to the side railings in a casual kind of way, to show that he could handle the danger, no problem.

He ran from the rails to the slide, then up and down the slide, then back to the merry-go-round in a dizzying performance of young male energy. Two girls watched silently from the edge of the playground. It was beautiful, this display of energy; it was everything I thought of when I thought of youth, yet I couldn't help but remember his elementary school teachers complaining endlessly of this very vigor.

Every now and then he'd look over to make sure I was watching, and I'd smile. I didn't want him to know how torn I was at his leaving, didn't want him to feel the dark thing already growing in my throat like some new infection.

I blinked back my grief, then suddenly it was really dusk and the whole field, every inch of it, came alive with the glowing bodies of thousands of fireflies, blinking their own spirit, searching for something kindred. Their light felt like a blessing, a consolation, a reminder of how beautiful the earth was, and Gray: *look at me, look at me, remember, remember this,* they seemed to blink. Their flashing lights were a reminder that what makes life beautiful is precisely the fact that it doesn't last.

The world looked upside down, as if the stars had descended to cover the earth for a time, to touch us with their smallest lights. May none of these be broken, I asked, may they stay whole until their short lives stop, may someone be there, sober and full of human light, watching over their sweet, boundless energy.

Yarn

I love to work with yarn that's hand-spun, hand dyed or painted by someone who loves wool, and cares for the animals who give it up to us—there's such loveliness in the unevenness of it, the unexpected variations in color as a strand slips through your fingers, its coarse silkiness, even though sometimes the spinner misses a twist, creates a weakness that will reveal itself in the finished product, the yarn thinning to almost nothing as you stitch a scarf or sweater, say. Sometimes you must cut the yarn, begin again with a healthier part of the strand. Other times, you miss the weakness and stitch it right into the garment, a flaw that doesn't show up until you put stress on it, and the whole row undoes itself.

Still, I prefer these yarns. They're nothing like synthetics, so reliable and predictable, each strand perfectly colored and twisted, easy to work with, machine washable to boot.

No, give me a bit of turbulence, the beauty of imperfection, this rough texture that hints at intimacy with sheep or llama or alpaca, give me the very real possibility that at any moment it could all unravel.

It's Come Undone: Crocheting and Catastrophe

. . . the human hand…has its own form of intelligence and memory.
—Elizabeth Zimmerman

Some of my earliest memories involve watching my mother crochet in our small living room nights when my father was away working his second job or out somewhere carousing. Oh, the bright and colorful afghans she made for her five children! Although I don't remember her smiling while she crocheted, she seemed more serene than at other times, centered, surrounded by balls of yarn, an afghan slowly taking shape in her lap. Sometimes she worked with granny squares, stacking up hundreds of multi-colored squares next to her on the sofa, then, months later, stitching them together in a lively design, making a whole of pieces in ways I'm sure she wished she could do with the broken bits of her life with my father.

Even as a child I perceived the swirl of chaos around my father, who often came home late from work, smelling funny and slurring his speech. I sensed my mother's crocheting was a way of creating a bit of calm in the frequent storms my father choreographed, storms that included strange women calling our house late at night, strange women's jewelry found in his car, increasing DUIs, car accidents and hospitalizations until, finally, just short of his 60th birthday, his liver in an advanced state of cirrhosis, he slipped into a vegetative state and died a few months later. In those years, I kept a journal and wrote poems in secret, which became my way of reflecting on my father's life, since my mother rarely talked about it unless forced. Instead of talking, instead of writing, she crocheted.

My mother has shared with me that crocheting all those years was, for her, a form of meditation. Instead of doing almost nothing, as in traditional meditation, with one's hands, hers were always moving, always in contact with the yarn she was looping and yarning over and pulling through in a rhythm I now understand, as a crocheter myself, underlies any thoughts scuttling about in your brain. Whatever else you might be thinking about while crocheting, you usually must be counting—*one single crochet front loop only; one back loop only, skip one stitch; three single crochets in the next stitch, repeat until you have 150 stitches.* Counting underlies all your thoughts in crochet, giving them a substance and song they might otherwise not have had.

If you're mourning some loss, as my mother often would have been—not only did she lose her husband over the years to other women and drink, but both her younger sister, and her troubled son, my brother, died young of drug overdoses—the yarn slowly but surely binds you to that loss. Maybe your stitches take on the shape of your grief, swelling as your eyes do, maybe you tighten them when angry or hold the tension a bit more loosely when you're sad. Maybe you're thinking of someone you love who's not lost but still alive, your focus to create something beautiful for him, to stitch your affection into the yarn.

While I grew to trust words to stitch the wounds in my heart, my mother preferred crocheting. The comfort of the ball of yarn next to you, the satisfaction of it growing smaller as your project takes on shape and dimension; the wonder of the colors as they reveal themselves in a stitch, especially when you have a skein of multi-colored or self-striping yarn; the rhythm of the changes of colors and of the stitching itself; the sensuous sliding of the hook into the opening of the stitch; the pulling and looping and yarning over; the comforting feel of the completed stitch; these are some of the reasons I imagine she came to love crochet.

I make my living now as a poet and teacher of writing, although I also crochet, and I can't help but see connections between writing and crocheting. When crocheting a long row of single crochets, the rhythm of it feels to me like a kind of poetic meter, an extended trochaic foot, one that slides around, has a bit of a southern accent maybe, with slightly too many syllables—enter, yarn over, pull, enter yarn over pull—. It feels as if you're weaving a poem. A row of crocheting is not unlike a line of poetry where foot and meter are important, the turning chain like the rhymed syllable of the last word of an iambic pentameter line. If you're working with color, the colors must echo and complement each other the same way words do in a poem or lyric essay.

I first turned to writing poems to find vessels to contain the chaos of the family into which I was born; poems offered a way to present a gift to the world that often came from those early days' tragedies. Crocheting has become a force almost equal to poetry as an expressive art for me, since both are creative acts that can be at once calming and transformative, both empowering in times of crises.

The truth is, of course, that women have often used fiber art—weaving, knitting or crocheting—as a tool for getting through difficult times. The earliest literary example we have might be Penelope, Odysseus' wife, who promises she will remarry once she finishes weaving a burial shroud for Laertes. During the day, she works on the shroud, but unravels it at night, hoping Odysseus will return before she is forced to marry one of her property-hungry suitors. This story also points out that it's not the product of the weaving that's important, rather the process itself.

Several recent books link crochet's older sister, knitting, to psychological and spiritual recovery. Ann Hood's memoir, *Comfort: A Journey through Grief,* and her novel, *The Knitting Circle,* to pick two of my own favorites, are both inspired by her own experience learning to knit to help recover from the unexpected death of her young daughter. Susan Gordon Lydon, in *Knitting Heaven and Earth,* writes about using knitting and needlework to heal from the grief of death as well as her own diagnosis of breast cancer. Likewise, crochet blogger Kathryn Vercillo's site, *Crochet Concupiscence,* is full of stories of many who crocheted their way through grief; she herself has written of how she crocheted her way out of depression.

My own drug of choice is crochet, not knitting, although most yarn stores, pattern magazines, and books privilege knitting. Crocheting is in my blood because that's the art my mother taught me, and it's what her mother taught her. I learned to hold a crochet hook around the same age I learned to wield a pen, and it feels as natural to hold a crochet hook as it does a pen.

Knitting and crocheting are sometimes confused, as they both involve yarn and may lead to similar projects: hats, scarves, gloves, sweaters, afghans, blankets. I often crochet in public—it's a great way to sit through bad poetry readings if you are not at liberty to leave—and am constantly responding to questions of "What are you knitting?" with *I'm crocheting.* Both arts involve manipulating loops of yarn, although knitters use two knitting needles, while crocheters employ a single tool, the crochet hook. Crocheters enjoy dozens of kinds of stitches; knitters have only two. Crocheting uses more yarn than knitting, and has more architecture. Running your hands along a crocheted item you'll feel the bumps of the stitch, which are in higher relief than those of knitting.

I now crochet as much, if not more, than my mother, and I'm grateful for her early lessons. I'm lucky to be able to afford the kinds of yarns my mother could not. I like to use kettle-dyed, natural yarn (as opposed to synthetics) for my crochet projects as I prefer the slightly coarser look and variegations in color; I like handspun yarns such as those from Malabrigo, a woman's collective from Uruguay, that vary in lovely ways both in the shades of the color of the yarn and in the diameter of the yarn itself so that it might be thick at one part and thin in another. As the yarn runs through my fingers I think of the animals or plants from which it came, and I feel more connected with the earth. I also like supporting the women in rural areas of South America, many of whom would live in poverty without the ability to make and sell this yarn.

Unfortunately, a love of crocheting is not the only thing I share with my mother. Like her, I also gave birth to a son who would grow into a troubled teenager, and whose journey, like my brother's, deeper and deeper into drugs and alcohol would dominate my waking hours for many years and haunt me in midlife even more than I was already haunted by the deaths of my brother and father.

Ten years ago, Gray, who was then nineteen and had been growing increasingly hostile to everyone who loved him during his teen years, took a turn for the worse, exhibiting a kind of emotional cruelty I can hardly bear, still, after all these years, to re-enter. He seemed to be spiraling into blackness; he'd dropped out of high school, refused to find work, and had been picked up on several occasions for public drunkenness and shoplifting. Hanging out with a crowd deep into hard drugs, one of his friends who regularly shot up heroin was so proud of it that he had taped needles onto his guitar. My son was jobless and living in my basement, although he had talked a doctor into giving him a prescription for Adderall so that he could get up in the mornings and look for a job, which he never did. I would sometimes find him and a girlfriend asleep in the basement in the mornings, emptied wine bottles on the floor, they unable to rise. I doled out the Adderall, one a day, until he visited his father, from whom I was divorced, in Texas, for a couple of weeks. He took the prescription bottle with him, and when I asked for it back on his return, he claimed to have lost it.

One night, when I was out of town and he was home alone, the garage caught fire and burned to the ground. The house itself was scorched on one side and could have also gone up with my son asleep inside, the fire-chief told me later, had someone who witnessed the blaze not called the fire department. The fire-chief also said my son had been so "inebriated" when he interviewed him about the fire he could hardly understand what he was saying. Years later Gray would confess that he and friends had had a party in the garage that night; they had all gotten drunk, and he'd fought with one of the friends, who had later set the garage on fire in retaliation. Much later, he would tell another friend of mine that he'd lit the fire himself.

When I returned home from my trip, in addition to the charred space where the garage used to be, I found bottles of beer stashed everywhere in the house, in record cabinets, clothes drawers, under beds. I found evidence online through chat boxes he'd left open on my computer that he'd been stealing copious amounts of cough syrup, wine and beer. He was advising friends on how to shoplift as well as how to mix drugs to achieve various kinds of highs. When I confronted him one afternoon about what I'd found, he called me a stupid fucking bitch, and locked himself in his room. Later that night I found a message he'd left for me on the desk top of my computer in about 32-point bold: **I HATE YOU. I HOPE YOU DIE.**

Not long after this confrontation he wound up in jail overnight because of a drunken fight that left him with two black eyes and, later, an altercation with a policeman while he was still drunk. That night, while he was in jail, one of his former girlfriends confessed to me how worried she was about him, his drinking, the drugs (specifically Adderall) she said he was doling out to friends, selling, and abusing it himself. She confirmed my suspicions that he had not lost the prescription bottle of Adderall.

The next morning the police informed me he still had so much alcohol in him that they could not even bring him in front of the judge for sentencing. They suggested one option to protect him might be to have him committed for drug and alcohol abuse. I suspected he would never forgive me for this act, but I also couldn't see that I had many other options.

While he was still sobering up in jail I submitted the paperwork to have him committed. I had to write on the commitment papers that I felt he was a danger to both himself and others. It was by far the most agonizing writing I have ever done, the most horrific paper I have ever felt it necessary to sign.

During his commitment, I began to crochet an afghan for him. I had crocheted on and off since I was a child, but this was the first time I'd taken it up almost out of desperation. I felt helpless; everything seemed so chaotic. I could hardly get a sentence out during visits to the hospital where he was being confined before he'd curse and tell me to go away. From the dark and angry place where he lived, he couldn't hear or receive my words or love. As a mother, this rejection was painful; as someone who had spent her life making poems and essays, stitching words, if you will, to speak, the failure of my own words made me feel wretched. I couldn't console even myself with words; the feeling of what was happening seemed so raw, I couldn't bear, then, to try to capture it in words. Even now, reliving those events to write this essay, is excruciatingly painful.

If I felt my words had no power then, or if I could find no way to bring them to power during those black times, if I couldn't seem to pick up a pen, I could still pick up a crochet hook. I could count rows, stitches. I could bear to think of what my son's life had become while I crocheted, the murmuring of my counting in the background.

And so I began crocheting for him, as my mother had for all her children so many years earlier. I made the afghan of colors I thought he would like in a pattern I thought he might like. The project kept me sane for the month he was in the hospital, and gave me something both aesthetic and sensible to do with my hands, my grief, my wordlessness. I couldn't solve his problems, but I could unscramble the design dilemmas of an afghan; I could hook him a gift that could stitch a mother's love into the silent weight and heft of yarn.

I chose worsted weight wool, the right weight for something you want to give warmth: a thick, but not chunky yarn. I don't remember the precise pattern or color scheme, but I do remember blacks, purples and yellows: in my mind, yellow for hope, black for grief, purple, one of his favorite colors. A repeating series of puff stitches that shaped large ovals that looked something like eyes. Even now, so many years later, I remember how satisfying it was to sit on my sofa in the evenings when it was very cold outside to work on this afghan. The snow falling, fire blazing in the fireplace, the afghan growing under my fingers, slowly, day by day. Sometimes I thought of my mother and all those nights she had crocheted while my father was drinking himself to death. I hoped some intervention would save my son from that fall, but I was beginning to feel all but powerless to help.

Once the pattern was ingrained in my fingers I didn't have to think about it so much; it felt at times as if I were in a trance, my fingers making the same movements over and over again: *Yarn over,* insert hook into the stitch; *yarn over,* pull through; *yarn over,* pull through again; *yarn over,* pull all loops off the hook; half double-crochet formed for the background. Three rows of that. Then the puff stitches: five yarn-overs and pull-throughs that made a stitch that puffed out, just as the name suggests. I crocheted through the nights and thought about my son. Yellow. *Yarn over, one.* Maybe he'll never speak to me again. *Insert hook into stitch.* It's not about you, Sheryl, it's about him. Maybe the forced twelve-step program will help. *Yarn over, two.* At least he isn't with the guy who tapes needles to his guitar. *Pull through.* How long will he be angry, will the meds help? *Yarn over three.* Are they treating him well? *Pull through.* What else could I have done. *All loops off hook.* Repeat for Black, Purple. And on and on, over and over, hundreds of rows, thousands of stitches.

When he was released from the hospital, he was required to continue in a twelve-step program, and to have a stable place to live. He stayed with me for a while in Iowa where we'd been living, then moved to Texas to be with his father, who bought him a beer for his 20th birthday, and so it started all over again, the drinking, the drugs, the anger. He stopped taking the medications that had been prescribed to him while he'd been in the hospital, where, in addition to drug and alcohol abuse, he'd been diagnosed with bipolar disorder.

After a few months he returned to Iowa, but not to stay with me. He avoided talking with me as much as possible, moving in with a new girlfriend I didn't trust and some other friends I also didn't trust. They lived in a falling-apart house with broken windows. I don't know how he managed money for the cigarettes he'd started smoking. He rarely visited, though he occasionally tolerated a short visit from me. I taught my classes during the day, numb, saw a therapist weekly, also numb, and worked on the afghan at nights, which was the only time I felt alive. Each time I picked up the hook and pulled the afghan on my lap I felt balanced, focused, a clear project in front of me. Sometimes this was the only time in the entire day I felt centered. If I lost attention and forgot to count I could rip a few rows out and start over. If I put my mind to it, though, if I focused only on the pattern, I could make a perfect row, which was something, given the ragged world into which I had fallen.

If I allowed feelings of hopelessness to take over while stitching (and I sometimes did), there were always the intensely beautiful colors of the afghan emerging in a pattern to remind me I was accomplishing something. Yellow, a field of goldenrod, purple the color of ripe eggplant, black, the darkness I was keeping at bay by stitching it into the afghan. The colors, the pattern, the design reminded me, over and over, with each stitch, that beauty might come out of grief.

When you feel hopeless, as if you can do nothing right, it's useful to have a reminder that you can engage in an activity that will grow into something of value. The long rows needed to make afghans allow you to sink into a soothing rhythm. There's nothing unexpected, no horrible blow-up, no yelling or screaming or fighting, just the hook moving in and out, in and out, reliable, steady, familiar as your breath. The thing taking shape, almost imperceptibly, under your fingers, an object whose colors and design you chose. Crocheting does not offer the oblivion of drink, which I sometimes also engaged in those days; it requires rather the opposite: engagement. Although I could not bring myself to write poems around this time, I kept up a journal, and crocheting allowed me quiet time to reflect. I may not have written much, but I meditated deeply, partly thanks to the act of sitting down every evening to work with my hands.

By the end of six weeks I had completed so much of the afghan that it covered the lower half of my body as I worked on it. The afghan began to keep me warm in ways I hoped it would eventually warm he who would not be spoken to.

At one point while I was still working on the afghan, my son, drunk and high, paid a surprise visit to his old girlfriend, the one who had shared with me her fears about his trajectory. She wouldn't let him into her apartment, so he kicked the door in. She called the police, but he got away before they arrived. A warrant was issued for his arrest. I learned from one of his friends that he was hiding from the police with the guy who had needles taped to his guitar. It was Christmas time. I had a bag of groceries and kitchen supplies under the tree for him.

One evening not too soon after the door incident, as I was sitting on the sofa crocheting, I saw, though the living room window, his current girlfriend's junker car pull up in front of the house. He and the girlfriend were sitting in the car smoking and talking. I only had a few minutes. I called a friend. *Please,* I said, *call the police, tell them he is outside of my house. I don't have time. Tell them to come get him.*

I hung up, and in a minute Gray came in. It was awkward. He didn't want to sit down. He just wanted to pick some clothes up, he said. We talked for five minutes, the Christmas tree lights twinkling, the fireplace blazing, the unfinished afghan on the sofa, the afghan he didn't even know was for him. At some point the doorbell rang and two policemen asked for my son. I pointed to him. He didn't resist. They put him in handcuffs and took him away.

I finish the afghan while Gray is in jail. I drive out to see him a few times, but after a while I stop, because he usually winds up telling me to fuck off.

Although I love designing crocheted items and I love the actual act of crocheting, I do not enjoy the finishing-off part. That is the part where you must weave in all the ends so that they don't come undone. If you've been working with yarns of different colors you may have lots of ends that need to be woven in. It's not exciting. It's not creative. There's no comforting rhythm because you're constantly starting and stopping at often-irregular intervals. You must use a tapestry needle to weave the ends in, threading it with the yarn ends you've left hanging where you changed or ran out of yarn. You weave in and out of the stitches, first one way and then the opposite way, and when you've woven enough so that it seems it would be impossible for the stitch to come to come undone, you snip the yarn and pull the stitch over it so that you can't see the work you've just done securing the stitch. It's tedious work, but it's something you need to do if you want your work to last and not come apart the first time you wash it.

Perhaps another reason I don't like weaving in the ends is because it means the project is almost finished; I've become intimate with this work, it's come alive under my hands and I've put a lot of myself into it. Now it will be done, finished, like a novel whose characters have drawn you in close for a time. To finish is to abandon them.

I gave Gray the afghan when he was released from jail. He moved back in with the girlfriend I didn't trust in the broken-down house with the broken windows, and I don't know if they used the afghan or not, but sometime later when I helped him move out of that place I found it stuffed in a black plastic bag. He said it had come partly undone and they hadn't known what to do with it.

I took the afghan home with me; it smelled like cigarette smoke and sour wine, but I repaired where it had unraveled and went back to re-check everywhere I had changed yarn to make certain it wouldn't unravel again. I washed it, checked it again, then folded it neatly and put it in my linen closet. I would give it back to him when he was settled in another place.

Today, ten years after Gray's initial release from jail, he still struggles with some of the same issues that got him into trouble when he was younger. He's returned to jail on several occasions for relatively minor issues, and admits to having a drinking problem, but he has a stable job that he likes and is relatively independent. We talk frequently and he asks and accepts advice. He tells me, sometimes, that he loves me. Although his moods vary widely, and he struggles, as I do, with depression, most of the time he no longer feels like a danger to himself or others.

I honestly don't know if the acts of having him committed and jailed helped. What I do know is that the time in the hospital and jail stopped for two short periods what seemed like a staggering fall that could have led to his death and perhaps those of others. What I do know is that crocheting the afghan was a good decision for me. I was able to keep balanced and even *spirited* in the sense of filling myself with something that felt spiritual in a dark time, through crochet. Idle hands may not necessarily be the devil's tools, as the saying goes, but idle hands certainly are the tools of listlessness, depression, and spiritual torpor. When I think of the afghan I made my son so many years ago, I feel a satisfaction I can hardly express that something both practical and beautiful came from sorrow and a sense of helplessness.

This year, I crocheted an alpaca hat and wool scarf for him for Christmas. The hat is made of soft brown baby alpaca, comfortable and slouchy, the yarn lustrous and silky. The yarn is so soft it feels like it will melt in my hands, and is exactly the color of his hair, a bright, hopeful brown. Alpaca is as soft as cashmere but stronger than wool. I made the hat of simple single crochets with intricate increases.

When I visited him over the Christmas holidays in Texas, where he now lives, he wore the hat the whole time after I gave it to him, and even slept with it on. He drank a lot while we were there and I could see he was depressed; at one point when we were alone together tears fell from his eyes as I was driving him to his father's house.

"I don't know what will become of me, Mom," he said, pulling the hat down around his ears.

I made the scarf in a gray yarn crocheted in a ribbed pattern with a thin row—quietly shocking—of multicolored yarn, with hues of turquoise, deep blues, reds and pinks. The idea for the scarf was inspired by Navaho weavers, many of whom include a "spirit line" in their blankets, a small strand of contrasting color that flows from the original design element to the outer edges. The line is there so that the weaver's creative spirit does not get trapped in the blanket, unable to make anything else. It is, if you will, a way out. As much love and hope as I might put into a scarf or hat or afghan, I don't want my own spirit trapped there. I want to be able to pick up a hook as I pick up a pen, over and over again, to write with yarn as I write with words, to not get lost, but to get out and start again somewhere else, yarning over and entering another stitch. It's not unlike the kind of writing I'm doing right now, a writing that causes one to have to descend or revisit some dark place, but to be able to come out of that place.

I also want to be able to *let go*, something my own work with twelve-step programs has taught, and so the spirit line for me is also a physical symbol that at the same time I'm making something for my son I'm also letting go of him. I'm not a super power, not a higher power, I'm only a mother whose role in his life will continue to recede as he ages.

The hat and scarf, like the afghan I made for him years ago, are kinds of prayers, ways of touching one who still, sometimes, will not let me touch him, one who, sometimes, is suspicious of words. The hat and scarf will warm him in ways I wish I could with my hands. Maybe, now, he can sense my crochet gifts to him as spirit-warmers as well as body-warmers.

Poet Pablo Neruda says that writing should be like bread, and I have always loved the idea that our words might feed one who could otherwise go hungry, that writing could be that necessary and elemental. But bread, once eaten, is gone, whereas an afghan, blanket or crocheted garment can be used over and over. So, of late I have been hoping that my writing can be as useful as a blanket made with my own hands. That this essay of woven words, in the hands of a reader, might delight, comfort and warm. That it be there, to return to, repeatedly, providing a safe space for reflection.

I don't want to think what might happen if my son doesn't stop drinking, I don't want to think how little I can influence his life. This hat, this scarf, each stitch a word in a prayer: *Keep-him-warm, keep-him-safe, keep-him.* I crochet words, wish, blessing and spell into the scarf, I make the hat a magic thing, like the cap of Hades, one that may make him invisible to the terrors of night. I hope my stitches will hook something words cannot. I crochet apology, regret; I crochet hope, I crochet sorrow, desire, rhythm, beauty. I weave in the ends, trust it won't come undone, and gift it, this talisman, this charm, this scar, beautiful, of catastrophe.

A New Kind of Poem

At some point your young adult children will stop wanting to talk to you. It's ironic that in an age of hyper communication, in an age where most young people carry cell phones as if they were extensions of their hands, you will call, you will text, you will email, you will post on their Facebook page, but you will not get a response. Months will pass with nothing but silence. The first time this happens you will fear that they have been in a horrible accident, you will visualize them in the hospital, suffering, having lost a limb, or worse, in a coma, unable to call. Maybe they are depressed, doing drugs, sleeping on the street.

At some point, maybe when they need something, they will call. They will say sorry mom, that I haven't responded to your messages, I was busy with my new job, or my computer has been broken, or they turned the electricity off at the house because we couldn't pay the bill, or my car died, or my phone died, or I didn't recognize this number was yours, or I stopped doing Facebook, or I don't check emails or voice messages or texts.

You can't help but think that if you were someone else, a close friend, someone around their age, or even a stranger, anyone, really, anyone but the mother, they would have picked up the phone, responded to the email or text, returned the voice message.

You are not sure at which point you should let go of wanting to hear your child's voice or see a message keyed in their own hands, but one day you wake up after months of silence again, and you get it, you see that this not-responding is actually a response of the highest order, a response not unlike a poem, a poem so compressed it's wordless, the imagery so transcendent it's invisible, the music so pure it's become silence, a poem of nothing and everything, cryptic and terrifyingly clear.

Leatherback Sea Turtle

Mother's Day, 2007

It's midnight, and we've trudged for several hours along the moonlit sands of a Costa Rican beach to find this dark, speckled lump in the sand, this ancient animal laying eggs just steps from the ocean. We see by moonlight how huge she is—bigger than any of us, a nine-hundred-pound mother who mated somewhere in the sea and is come down under cover of night to lay eggs. Caught in the birthing trance, she won't notice our witness until she's done: it's all she can think of, this giving birth.

Her huge body quivers, and she moans as she lays egg after egg after egg—over a hundred by the end of it. Each egg she lays is taken by a man lying between her legs, a thief with a good heart; he'll bring them to the hatchery to protect them from predators, human and other, the ones that have brought her to this very place, *endangered*.

I'm with students. I've brought them here wanting them to see something real, something they'll never forget, something that will live in them forever, and I keep telling myself the man with the red lamp on his head, the man between her legs, is a good guy, that most of her eggs would never hatch without our help into this world we have caused to change so much. But I wish it hadn't come to this.

She's about thirty years old, the guide tells us, and I think suddenly of what day it is, and of my son from whom I am estranged, and who was born when I was thirty. The guide tells us we can touch her, and I do, I stroke her leathery back and muscled flippers, and take her rich, fetid, ocean-sweet smell into me, and soon, because she doesn't know all her eggs are gone, she starts to move her flippers in the sand trying to bury what is no longer there, her last act as a mother to protect what she will never see. Trusting the nest she's built is a good one, that the sun will warm the eggs and her babes make it to the sea when it's time, she'll soon leave and make her own way back.

I look out at the ocean, the night and stars, suddenly sad. Mother's Day is a stupid day, I tell myself, a day for restaurants and florists and card companies, a day of forced acknowledgement of the One who gave birth to us and did not leave. My son, as usual, will not call or send flowers, a card or even a text on this day—and I wish I didn't care.

I long to be like this turtle I've fallen in love with. If only we could mother like her: make a nest in the safest place we know, lay our eggs, cover them as best we can, then turn around, lumber back into sea and our solitary lives, never looking back.

To Drink a Glacier

Juneau lies on a thin strip of land at the mouth of Gold Creek amidst a backdrop of mountains and glaciers that push down from the Juneau Ice Fields, which native people called "Home of the Spirits." The irony of this name is not lost on me; I've seen a lot of public drunkenness since arriving in Alaska two months ago. I came here hoping to find a nourishing wildness of land, but the real discovery I've made is of its darker, more familiar, sister—the wildness of hard drinking in the towns that make up the frontier to America's last wilderness. It's quite a surreal landscape: the wildly drunk drunks, sometimes native, sometimes not, stumbling about the most beautiful land I've ever seen. I'm reminded that the old label for what we now call alcoholism is dipsomania, which means "crazy with thirst." As I hammer—with difficulty—the final tent stake into this rocky soil, I wonder if the thirst I have for wildness and for union with the land, is not more deeply connected to my own thirst for alcohol than I have wanted to admit. Carl Jung would write that the alcoholic's craving for alcohol is the equivalent, on a low level, of a spiritual thirst for wholeness, a desire for union with whatever one understands as God. My stomach grumbles—it's time for dinner—and I decide this is way too heavy to think about right now, given the state of my hunger and the beauty of the glacier.

I've made camp near Mendenhall Glacier, which is eleven miles northwest of Juneau. The Mendenhall is twelve miles long and, in places, one-and-a-half miles wide. It was formed during the Little Ice Age that peaked in the seventeenth and eighteenth centuries. It's retreated two and a half miles during the last 230 years, and is currently retreating at the rate of fifty-seventy feet a year. John Muir wrote of this glacier in 1879 that it was "one of the most beautiful of all the coastal glaciers that are in the first stage of decadence." This glacier, like some of the people who call it home, is dying.

I'm camped about forty feet from Mendenhall Lake, which is where the glacier terminates. Chunks of ice fallen from the glacier are visible in the lake, though I've not seen or heard any chunks breaking off from the glacier. Glaciers are rivers of ice, though you can't see the ice moving in the way you can see the waters of a river flow. The Mendenhall is moving at the rate of two feet a day, though it's melting faster than its moving, which is why it's said to be retreating.

Once enough snow and ice has accumulated in an area, the pressure causes the snow on the very bottom to undergo a structural change into a dense form of ice called glacier ice. As that ice begins to accumulate, gravity causes the whole mass to move downhill. As it moves, it scrapes the earth's surface, picking up rocks and other sediment along the way. A retreating glacier, such as the Mendenhall, leaves behind that rock and sediment. This deposit is called glacial till, and is made up mostly of ground-up rock; there's hardly any organic content. It's interesting to walk around the base of a retreating glacier because you can see, as you walk toward the glacier, that the plant forms become more primitive the closer they are to the glacier. Only limited organisms, such as lichens and mosses, can grow in the newly deposited glacial till. Eventually, though, pioneer plants like fireweed take hold and start to improve the soil for other species. Then low shrubs and broadleaf trees, such as willow and alder, take root and improve the soil even more. Finally evergreens move in and develop into forest.

The receding glacier thus provides a new beginning for everything. The slate's been wiped clean, everything is forgiven, and we get to start all over again. The landscape of my birthplace, Louisiana, doesn't allow for that; our winters are so mild, nothing ever gets totally wiped out. The southern wetlands are rich areas for flora and fauna, but we can never utterly begin again. As if there's too much history, the Southern swamp filled with the weight of too much knowledge that can never be scraped away or hidden under tons of ice.

It's very late but there's still enough light in the sky to see the top of the glacier from where I sit in front of my tent, bundled up, drinking the last of the wine. How familiar, how, yes, *intimate* glaciers are with the earth; the glacier touches the earth in precisely the way I'd like to touch it, a touching that is physical medicine for the bloodless abstractions we sometimes allow to infest us. The glacier takes its shape as well as gives shape to the land it covers in the same way long married couples shape each other.

It is not glaciers but swamps that have shaped me, the swamps and dark waters of the urban Deep South, which is another landscape that has given birth to a great number of alcoholics, many of my relatives among them. I have made this trip alone because I wanted to get away from the swamp of my family and their seductive addictions, but I also made the trip because I wanted to do something brave. Spending several months alone camping in Alaska seemed like a brave thing for a woman like me, born and bred in New Orleans, to do. As I douse the lantern and climb into my sleeping bag it also occurs to me that having been fed the importance of female beauty as a young girl, I now want to go somewhere, to do something where traditional, mostly Southern, notions of beauty will not help me survive. So that when that detested beauty fails me it won't matter in the slightest. I have not escaped the specter of alcoholism that somehow seems tied to both states, though, and I will have to ask myself, eventually, why I brought so many bottles of wine with me on this trip.

The smell of pine and the chill of the glacier-kissed air enter me like aphrodisiacs. I breathe in the air and sigh, as if this place had touched me just where I want to be touched. Conventional wisdom says that women reach their sexual peak in mid-life; the fierce rushing waters of the glacial falls I saw earlier today remind me of the desire I feel flooding me these days, unasked for, and sometimes unwanted. As I wrestle with the sleeping bag full of nothing but myself, it occurs to me that there's something wondrous about being female and middle-aged. I, like the glacier falls, am exhibiting a spectacular melting, that great show of last power signifying the brilliant autumn of a woman's life. Can I learn to take comfort in sharing this melting with the non-human lover on whose back I've placed my bed?

It was so cold last night that neither the wine nor my down sleeping bag kept the chill from creeping into me. I'm camped right at the base of the glacier, so the air here is much colder than that of the city proper. The cold entered me violently, as if it owned me, or wanted to.

I woke this morning from a strange dream about my younger brother, who died a few years ago at a young age of a drug overdose. In the dream, he appeared at my campsite skeletal, but still handsome. I had been staring at the glacier, and his shape appeared out of the glacial ice. I wonder again about the meaning of "home of the spirits." I understood, in the dream, that my brother was still dead, but that he was somehow able to move and speak. His eyes were cold, really cold, not just in the way they looked, but in the way they felt. I invited him in, fixed dinner for him, then asked him how Death had been treating him. Before he could answer I picked up a steak knife and cut out my heart. I placed it, glistening and throbbing, into his hands, and asked him to tell me what it meant to be alive. I woke up to the vicious cold of the glacial air before he could answer.

Even in a dream, it's an extreme act to cut out your heart and give it to someone. The act itself a powerful metaphor for what we do in search of intimacy. We speak often of "giving our hearts" to someone, but this dream brings home the violence and self-mutilation implied in the phrase. The darker side of that giving is muted in the way we understand the expression "giving your heart" because it's become so clichéd that no one hears the words and what they point to anymore.

The question I asked my brother in the dream—"what does it mean to be alive"—is what I ask this glacier, too, this glacier that's been alive thousands of years, and is now receding, now in the process of dying, losing more of itself to the earth as the years progress. It's a death that's life-giving, though, leaving moraine, water, everything good, behind. A death that's also a blessing. Maybe it's not right to call it a death, but rather a transformation. A transformation not unlike the one I'm undergoing now, the individual gray hairs beginning to light up my head, my breasts weakening and falling more and more towards the earth, as if with a hunger to be there, or to be joined with it.

After coffee and cereal with milk near to souring, I drive into town for some supplies. On the way out of the supermarket I see a phone and decide, out of the blue, to try to call an old friend, Bruce Braden, whom I know to have moved to Alaska some years ago. He, my ex-husband and I were housemates fifteen years ago. I haven't seen him for twelve years. I hadn't known what town he lived in, but I asked the Alaska operator if she could check the entire state for a Bruce Braden, and she found him in a small town just north of Anchorage.

It was great to talk to him. I haven't had a sustained conversation with a human in over a month, and I took great joy in the give and take of discussion. I remember Bruce as a driven, serious sort. He'd work hours and hours overtime, and because of job-related stress, used to have trouble with stomach ulcers. He had majored in journalism, and was doing photography and production work in Austin when I first knew him. I remember odd things about him, that he used to get up early and go duck hunting, that he liked dogs and dope, and that at a wedding once, when we were both drunk, he gave me a long, deep kiss. He's from Lubbock, and speaks with a heavy Texas accent. Once, after talking to my mother on the phone and falling back into the New Orleans-speak she always brings out in me, that "whea ya at dawlin" stuff, Bruce lectured me about my accent: "People are gonna layf at you if you tawk lahk that," he said, in his own lovely Texas accent.

He said he'd come to Alaska because of the stress of the life he was living—production manager for a commercial media company—and because he loved dogs. He and Sara, his wife, had visited Alaska for Sara's fortieth birthday and decided, after just a few days, to move here. They returned to Austin, put everything they had up for sale, and moved. Bruce is now doing landscaping, just to make ends meet, working about fifty hours a week (he'd work a hundred, he says, if he could, but there's never that much work). Sara spends six months of each year in Austin, working. They still have some bills, including a mortgage for a condo in Austin that they're finding hard to sell, which is why Sara must stay there working half the year making the kind of money she could never make here.

Bruce has thirty-five dogs—some are pets, some are his sled dogs—and he spends every moment he can working them. He's run, at least once, the Iditarod, the 1,200-mile annual sled-dog race from Anchorage to Nome. The Iditarod race is considered one of the most strenuous events in the world. There's below-zero temperatures most of the way, fierce winds, and all the hazards that go with crossing the most remote parts of Alaska in winter. Bruce's dream, and the real reason he is here, is to work to win it.

The Iditarod is usually run in March, and attracts about sixty or so of the world's best mushers, each with a team of up to twenty dogs. There's a top prize of $50,000, but the top mushers can spend $70,000 or more just to get their dogs into the race. And a lead dog can sell for over $8,000. The fee to race the Iditarod is over $1,000 per musher. Bruce must work hard to find sponsors to help him afford to make a run.

He got most excited when he was talking about dog-sledding itself. I was trying to tell him how moved I was to just be in the presence of a glacier when he laughed and said there's nothing like being behind a dog sled, the only sound the *shhh* of the sled, no one around for miles and miles. He goes for ten hours at a time. Says he'll take me if I come to visit.

After I hung up with him I tried to get a flight out to Anchorage to visit for a couple days, but the cost of a ticket at this late date was prohibitive. I decide I'll call him back tomorrow to let him know the bad news.

That a fever of sorts gets hold of one here. I could sense it in Bruce's voice when he was trying to explain to me why he came here, and I can feel it in myself. It goes beyond the bounds of reason. Robert Service: "It grips you like some kind of sinning."

I filled several water jugs last week with water from the glacial falls near Skagway. I reach for one of the jugs as soon as I unload the car with the supplies I picked up in town. I've developed a real thirst for this water, not unlike my thirst for wine. As I bring the jug to my lips and drink I'm aware that this water is possibly over a thousand years old. It's the sweetest, purest water I've ever tasted, which says something for old age. It looks like liquid silver and feels, as it moves through me, like a kind of healing potion, some *gris-gris* drink from that Witch of all witches, Nature. I feel heady with the pureness of it, almost intoxicated. This is the mother of all wines, wine before we knew wine. It is mouth and nipple to all waters, east or west, even that river I know as so tainted, the Mississippi where it wraps around New Orleans. If I close my eyes I can feel myself back to the falls, kneeling, cupping my hands and dipping them into the water that rushes like arterial blood from the wound in its ice-white skin. I bring the water to my lips and drink. That drink is like a kiss, a kiss that takes in the entire body of the other. To drink is the most physical of acts, to feel the body of that other touching our lips then entering our mouths like some wondrous omnipotent liquid tongue, touching our own tongue all over, the roofs and sides of our mouths, then moving in us and through us to where it knows, in its wisdom, it must, to touch every cell of the body. I hold the water in my mouth as if it were a fine wine, or the blood of a god before I swallow, trying to make the spiritual, sexual sweetness of it last. It doesn't have the tingle of wine, but it warms me nonetheless.

Robinson Jeffers would write some years ago that we had become "a little too abstract, a little too wise." I might add: A little too untrusting, a little too cynical, a little too paranoid. To drink this water is to submit to the earth instead of manipulating it, to trust the nonhuman other in the way, before AIDS, we could trust the body of the human other. I kneel to gather and drink water from a river of glacial melt, believing that water to be pure. This kneeling and drinking is a form of prayer, which is also a form of trust. To drink is to pray, to have faith in this water to heal us, to ask for the water's blessing and wisdom, to trust that it will nourish, not poison us.

Among all the disasters predicted as the planet warms this is the worst for me: the loss of the glaciers and their holy water. When we can no longer trust our waters, will we all become like the inhabitants of that city which gave birth to me, the city that's the last to see this water after it's passed through the belly of this continent and is no longer pure? Since the earliest days of the settlement of New Orleans more water-borne diseases afflicted its inhabitants, twice as much cholera as any other urban area. Thousands of people died because of "swamp miasma," noxious elements in the diseased water that threatened its inhabitants. People came to distrust the water so much they drank wine instead of water. Sometimes I wonder if this is one reason why the rate of alcoholism is so high in New Orleans.

No one would now dare drink the unpurified, unfiltered, untransformed water of the Mississippi, or that of long-polluted Lake Pontchartrain, or the water of any of the bayous and swamps and lakes that once were pure as this glacial water. Will we eventually lose our taste for that which is pure? Will we develop, as many of us have, even more of a taste for that most altered and most changed of waters? May we not, I say to the unspeaking glacial air with which I share the tent, may we not, I say, even though a bottle of chilled wine waits outside my tent for me to finish this reverie, may we not, I say, wondering if I am not lost already, but wanting it not to be so, may we not, may we not.

What would a glacier say if it could speak? Is its movement, its slow melting, a kind of speech? When I drink its waters am I drinking its language? Is it silly to wonder if it has some sort of awareness of its dying, its loss of itself? The glacier, I now realize, gave me the dream I had of my brother last night; they, the glacier and my brother, have something in common I need to understand. What is it? Loss, maybe. Will thinking about loss help me to know what it means to be alive?

I call Bruce to tell him I can't visit until maybe the winter. We talk for a long time. He reveals that he has a drinking problem, that the first thing he does in the morning is drink, that he drinks all day, especially the months his wife is gone. The darkness, the loneliness, gets to him. Says Sara doesn't even realize he has a problem, that I'm the first person to whom he's admitted it. His voice, so strained, thick with grief.

Everything Bruce said, as we continued to talk about his drinking, entered and found its mate in me, like a kind of unwelcome rhyming. I understand very well how loneliness can drive one to drink. The land itself is not enough. The land cannot save us. Beauty cannot save us. We must save ourselves. We need strength in ourselves to withstand the kind of extreme isolation one can find here. Perhaps that's the heroism I need but for which it sometimes seems I lack the courage. To carry solitude with grace and without drink.

John Haines, whose essays on his life in Alaska as a homesteader and trapper have moved me a great deal, writes: "It's good to know, though scorned and damned by the saviors of humankind, that a few durable things can still be counted on: whiskey, the solace of the poor, the outcast and the aging, the last religion." When there's no god to believe in, no great love to touch you to the core of your being, there is, at least, the warmth, security, and yes, holiness of drink. That beloved which is always faithful, always there. It's no mystery that Christ's blood is offered to us in the literal and metaphoric form of wine, and it's no mystery that alcoholics are such spiritually thirsty people.

I talked to Bruce a little about my brother's addiction and death, my father's alcoholism and death and my own drinking. If I am not yet alcoholic,

I could be there tomorrow, given the history of it in my family, and given the way I sometimes use alcohol to numb pain, to forget, to become someone else.

There's an otherness I feel enter me when I drink that's not unlike the otherness I feel when I walk into wild landscapes.

It's two days since I spoke with Bruce, and I've been spending most of the time hiking, though I'm still struggling with the sadness I feel at his predicament, trying to make sense of it while all this beauty surrounds me. I'm hiking the West Glacier. It's a lonely trail that hugs Mendenhall Lake but winds mostly through the forest, so you can't see much of the lake, though the diamond-blue top of the glacier is visible most of the time. Perhaps because of the freshness of my talk with Bruce the most dramatic elements of this landscape for me are the cuts and gashes in it, the scars and wounds of mountain and earth and ice where its blood-water flows so sweet and pure, leaving behind flashes of naked rock, unmelted ice, the emerald brilliance of trees and the occasional delicate swath of flowers.

I see a black bear on the trail. It's a small one, just below me on a switchback, and for a moment I think it's going to run towards me. It stares at me for a long few seconds. A rush of adrenaline, my heart pounding, the bear runs off into the woods, but my heart continues to throb the rest of the way up the glacier. I was scared, almost frozen with fear, but it was also a good feeling. I felt so alive, so close to the glacier, the world. Strangely like the feeling I have drinking the glacier water; here are two intimacies, one born of a sense of nurturance, one born of fear. It occurs to me that maybe you need to feel the presence of both to feel truly in the wild. And I'm beginning to think that the presence of another human need not interfere with the experience. I feel Bruce with me.

I make it to the end of the trail. I've been hiking for about five hours. In front of me is the glacier, white, with dark specks of soil and rock embedded in the ice. Several dark blue crevasses stare out at me like slit eyes or deep scars you can see inside of—they get purer and bluer the deeper you consider them. Sometimes a small, intense waterfall surprises you from the inside. Crevasses are wedge-shaped cracks or fissures formed by tensile stresses set up by ice movement. As humans break down under stress so too do glaciers. I walk over to one and look into it. I'm a little scared of falling in—it would be sure death—but it's so beautiful I keep inching closer and closer to the edge. The crevasses are the glacier's wounds it bares to us, sloe-eyed wounds that, when we gaze into them, offer a kind of terrifying intimacy with the nonhuman world. It's almost like gazing into Medusa's eyes.

What would happen were we to open our own wounds to the earth like that, bare them as this glacier does? Maybe, when we looked deeply at them, we might find something astonishing, like a hidden waterfall. Or not. Maybe just a vertical cave of ice, a death-slide that, when covered with snow gives the appearance of stability and sucks us in. Maybe death by freezing, a consequence of having gazed into the Gorgon's eyes.

I read a story of a woman's son who had climbed one of the glaciers near here. According to his companions, he was "dancing" on the glacier when he fell inside a crevasse and died. He had told his mother not to worry if he was ever killed while glacier climbing, that she should know he died happy.

I want this, to die happy. I want Bruce to die happy. Not drunk. Happy. Happy and high, high with the work of climbing a glacier, a mountain, running a dogsled.

I'm right next to the waterfall now, and can hear its lovely rushing, which sounds like many people whispering in some language I can't understand. I've walked, gingerly out on the glacier, which looks for all the world like a slow frozen river, ripples and all. Perhaps the beauty of the glacier has something to do with this tension between movement and stillness. Here, frozen, is the power of a river, which is all about movement. Such stillness, and but for the voice of the falls, such quiet. The glacier does its work in silence and darkness. Muir would write that glaciers "brood" over rocks. It is a dark work, the work of glaciers, but it's also a work of creation; because of them mountains are brought forth, land is scraped out for meadows, lakes, forests. Glaciers do the work of god in creating the world. Is it going too far to see them as gods? Perhaps this is what native people were thinking when they called the ice fields that birthed this glacier *home of the spirits*.

I kneel next to the waterfall, cup my hands, dip them into the water and bring them to my lips. I drink, and as I drink I close my eyes, try to feel the glacier's quiet inside me, to feel how my own brooding is like this glacier's. But what comes to me, as I swallow, is not quiet, but the way Bruce's voice sounded on the phone, as open as these crevasses and their hidden waterfalls:

> *I am so glad you called, Sheryl, so very really really glad.*

Note:

I kept in touch with Bruce for a few years after returning from Alaska, then we lost contact again. In January 2011, I tried to locate him and found instead a notice of his death. He died right before Christmas in 2009 at his home in Alaska, which had caught fire in the middle of the night. His wife was able to escape; he was not. He was 54. The obituary mentioned his love of mushing and dogs, that he was assistant Scout Master for the First Methodist Church Wasilla, Alaska scout troop, and that for the past ten years he and his wife were the coordinators for the Knik 200 qualifying race for the Iditarod or Yukon Quest races.

The Call of Bagpipes

Excuses

Say you were nervous, your husband's ex-wife was coming for dinner, your new stepchildren were going to be there, you were cooking and started with the wine too early, say you like to drink wine while cooking and didn't realize how much you were drinking, say everyone stayed too long and you didn't realize how much you were drinking, say you don't like being around lots of people and drinking makes it easier, say you are more interesting when you drink, say everyone else is more interesting when you drink, say an old friend was visiting and you didn't realize how much you were drinking, say everyone else was drinking, you were just trying to keep up and didn't realize how much you were drinking, say you feel like dancing when you drink, say you were preparing for a date and wanted to feel sexy, say you were sad because you hadn't heard from your son in a long time, or upset because you'd had an argument with a friend or had a bad day in general. It was raining, snowing, sleeting, too hot, too cold, say you wanted to celebrate your birthday or someone else's birthday, say it was Thanksgiving or St. Patrick's Day or Valentine's Day or just a regular day when you felt lonely or happy. Say you had a bad day writing or teaching, say you didn't realize you'd drunk the whole bottle, say surely you hadn't drunk the whole bottle, say you're sure there's still some left.

Denials

Don't believe it when your teenage son says you sometimes slur your words, don't believe it when your husband and ex-husband say it. Swear you would have noticed if you'd been slurring. Tell them to tape you next time. Feel triumphant when no one takes you up on it. Tell yourself blackouts are normal, it's fine not to remember things as long as it's only a few times a year, even blackouts are okay in moderation. You're productive at work, impeccably sober when you need to be, what does it matter what you do at home? You usually only drink a couple of glasses of wine to unwind, so it's okay to sometimes drink until you're sick; throwing up gets the poisons out, and if it's only once or twice a year, nothing to worry about. You're not a public drunk like your father.

It doesn't really matter that you have Hepatitis C, that your liver is weakened and your doctor's said you should stop drinking, because you found a nurse who told you a glass of wine every now and again would be okay, and anyway there's no real proof that drinking will make your liver any worse than it already is. And you have lived long enough, you tell yourself, do you really need to live another thirty years? Wouldn't twenty be enough? What does it matter if your liver shorts out a bit early? You don't want to be stumbling around at 80, right?

What To Call Yourself

Someone who likes to drink a lot, someone who knows how to hide how much she drinks, someone who's very good at hiding how much she drinks, someone who misses alcohol as you would miss the kindest, most forgiving mother in the world. A drinker, a wine lover. Someone who's forgotten where the off button is. Daughter, granddaughter of a drunk.

When you finally stop drinking, say you are allergic to wine, say it makes you sick, say you're taking some kind of medicine that doesn't mix well with it, say *not tonight*, say *maybe later*, say *not now*, say *sorry*, say you can't, say *no not even a little*, say *no, not even champagne*, say *no, not even a taste of your fine cognac, your special home-made in France wine, your grand cru whatever*, say you don't know the meaning of a little.

The Basement

One morning you wake to find yourself unusually sore. You get up to make coffee and find bruises on your wrists. Your husband isn't speaking to you at first. When you hand him his coffee he says *you don't remember last night, do you?* And you do remember, some of it, you remember you cooked dinner for 12 people, you remember you started cooking around 4:00 p.m., started drinking around 5:00, and that at some point after dinner when everyone was still hanging around you sensed you'd had too much and excused yourself to go to bed. You had thought you were being mature, you had thought it best to retire rather than be told later that you were slurring your speech or that you did something for which you might be ashamed. You had been proud of yourself: this was the key, you thought, just go to bed when it seems like you've had enough.

But now your husband tells you that you woke up later, walked downstairs naked, to the first floor and then down into the basement. Everyone was gone, he says, but can you imagine if they had all still been there (his ex-wife, his grown children). You kept wanting to go down, he says, you kept looking for stairs that went from the basement into the earth, stairs that didn't exist. He tried to get you to go upstairs but you yelled at him, he says, you told him to leave you alone, then, after a futile search for the stairs that would take you further down into some unimaginable darkness you began to climb back up to the second-floor bedroom, but then you started to fall down the stairs. He grabbed you to break the fall, he says, thus the bruises. You remember nothing, not the waking, not the walking, not the wanting to descend deeper into the earth, not the falling, not the grabbing.

Somehow this story makes you feel worse than the ones from when you were much younger, the ones when you woke up with someone whose name you didn't remember, having forgotten every word that had passed between you, every intimacy. Then, it was just regret that you'd had sex with this person you'd wanted to sleep with so much, this person to whom you were so deeply attracted; you'd had perhaps wonderful earth-moving, ecstatic sex, but you remembered nothing, no kiss, no touch, no undressing, no whispered words, nothing.

You wonder how much deeper you might have tried to go if your husband hadn't been there to stop you, if you would have clawed at the cement or found the ax and tried to chop out a hole to reach that bottom you seemed so hell-bent on reaching.

You don't really know what makes this time so much more special than any other time, but within a day you've decided. You will not walk naked and oblivious again on any fucking steps, you will not try to dig your way to more fucking darkness, you will not fall down another set of steps without being fully conscious, you will not fall, yet, into any fucking good night.

Eighteen Months Later

It's spring, and you're in a remote mountain village in the south of France. You're soaking in a bathtub full of lavender bubbles, a bar of violet-scented soap at hand. You're looking out of this many-windowed 12th century chateau at the valley below, the mountains, the rain that's pouring down, the lightening that's sometimes illuminating everything, listening to the thunder that's barking across the valley, the rain pounding the trees and the creek below. You are wishing, as you have wished every day for the last year and a half, that you had a glass of wine, just one, something white and maybe a little buttery, a chardonnay or maybe something lighter, sweeter, a good Riesling, something like summer, which is almost here. But you will not have a glass of wine, at least not today, although you are in a country that loves wine, although this valley and the one next and the one next are filled with ripening grapes that will be made into wine that you will not have.

You will drink nothing that will make this bath seem more than what it is: the bubbles just bubbles, the scent lavender and violet, nothing more, nothing less. The rain is rain. No wine will make it seem better or worse or something else. The thunder will roar as thunder does. No glass of wine will help you smile, relax you enough so that you can feel more than you do at this very moment: how lucky you are to be here, atop a mountain in a 12th century chateau with lavender bubbles and violet soap watching a thunderstorm develop under your eyes.

When you get out of the bath and dry off, when you look at your body in the mirror, no glass of wine will make it seem more or less than what it is, the body of an ordinary older woman. Sober, you will dry yourself off, dress, and open the windows wide so that you can smell the rain, the grass and the trees, hear more clearly the voice of the thunder, the rushing of the creek, drunk with rain.

You Think You Have Become Anti-Social

since you've stopped drinking. Parties no longer interest you, not even dinner parties, where everyone lingers too long and drinks wine while you sit there wanting to go off and read or write or play video games or check email or just about anything rather than sit here socializing with people who are drinking. You don't understand anymore why people just don't eat, have coffee or tea, and then go home. You wish they would go home. Even here, at this writer's retreat in the south of France, everyone gathers to drink wine at night. You can hear them, under your window, laughing and talking. You don't join them. At night you sleep well. They do not, and you want to tell them that they might sleep better if they didn't drink as much, but you keep your mouth shut because you know this is about you, not them. Your husband sometimes joins them, and sometimes he comes back to the bed a bit tipsy. He leaves bottles of wine in the room, sometimes full, sometimes empty. You try not to care, you tell yourself this is your problem, not his, but the bottles bother you, and the drinking bothers you and sometimes you hate yourself—what kind of boring, judgmental person have you become? Your husband is mostly loving and affectionate but you don't understand how he doesn't see that you have this sleeping monster inside of you, that you're doing your best to keep it down, but it's snarling, raging, and you don't know how he can't hear.

Lo Camin de la Ceba

It's windy and threatening rain, but that hasn't stopped them. Today, May 15th, is the day of the ancient onion walk from Mazamet, a village some twenty kilometers away, to this one, Labastide Esparbairenque. Every year for as long as anyone can remember, the Occitan villagers have walked to Labastide to buy onion plants, then stayed until evening to drink and eat, play music and dance. You gather with them now outside the village church of St. André, where the wind is bossing everyone around, but no one is leaving.

The sound of bagpipes fills the valley. A few villagers are playing the *crabas*, bagpipes made from whole skins of white goats. When they blow, the bodies seem to come alive again, grow fat, almost whole, headlessly piping drone and melody at once. There's nothing, *nothing*, like the sound of a bagpipe. The drone echoes without interruption like a sweet, deep melancholy you don't want to let go of, an unexpected rhyming, a vibrating in sinew and bone, a sudden and lingering breath, an awareness in the muscles of heart and eye, an *ohhhhhhmmmmmmmm* that will not be ignored, and you wonder what insight or madness you might come to if you listened long enough to the drone of a bagpipe. Against it, the chanter pipes its brave and clear melody. The two sounds, one like a dirge, one like a dance, speak as one voice, one instrument, the only instrument you know that has two such different voices.

There's free wine, and someone is grilling sausages. Someone else is frying potatoes, someone else selling bread and crepes. A woman is selling honey made from mountain acacia, thyme soap and chestnut butter, and someone is, of course, selling onion plants. Groups of families are spread out on blankets all along the mountain in the shadow of the church and its cemetery. Children and dogs are running everywhere, stealing sausages from each other as the *crabas* fill every unspoken-for cranny of this valley with drone and melody. Old ladies in church dresses smile, stand straight and proud with the help of canes. French men with red berets sit, drinking wine and smoking, some speaking French, some Occitan. On one side of the church laughing families, on the other, the cemetery for their dead. The two voices of the bagpipe seem appropriate for both picnic and funeral.

You wander among the living, *part* of you happy to be here, *part* of you feeling blessed to be among these friendly, wine-drinking folk. You buy onion plants and honey, chestnut butter. You chomp down on a French bread sausage sandwich, listening with both glee and sadness to the goat-pipes. Anyone who doesn't feel both the urge to dance and the urge to cry when listening to bag pipes is not really listening.

The other part of you, the darker one, comes alive whenever you walk past the free wine. *You could have one,* she says, *just one, look how small the glasses are, no one knows you're here, no one would know, no one.* She's not happy, the dark one, with anything, not the honey, not the soap, not the sausages or bread or the hopeful onion plants you have stuck into the coat of your jacket. She doesn't like the music, she doesn't like the people, the church or the cemetery, she only wants one thing, *just one.*

Later, you will walk home with your onion plants, the honey, chestnut butter and your miserable dark self. You will walk away from the festival, away from the music, through the ally of thousand-year old cypresses that leads toward your summer home here. You crumple into bed, exhausted with listening, exhausted with the effort of not drinking.

Eighteen months, you say to the dark one, as you try for sleep, *eighteen months it's been. When will you leave me alone.*

You sleep, finally, rolling, during the night over onto the onion plants you'd thrown onto the bed. In your dreams you hear the call of the bagpipes. Everything smells like onions, even the breath of the dark one, who visits you, as always: *I'll never leave you*, she drones, *I'm unending, without pause, without yield, without period. I'm you. I'm here for good.*

Play whatever melody you like.

The Third Step

---

*Made a decision to turn our will and our lives
over to the care of God as we understood Him.*
—The Big Book of Alcoholics Anonymous

My friend's son was killed last week. A young soldier, having fought in Afghanistan, he'd come home for a time, and was waiting to be deployed again in a few days. He was a man who loved the army, so his mother and the obituaries would say. He took his motorcycle out last Tuesday to visit the wife and child of a friend and fellow soldier still in Afghanistan. Perhaps it was a sunny day like this one, a blue sky, a spring day when trees are budding and the first fragile flowers blooming, close to the ground; perhaps it felt like a day of hope. A day he intended to comfort his friend's wife, to assure that her husband would return.

He was a good man like that, so his mother said, so the obituaries said, a man kind to children, though he had none. He'd been travelling on his motorbike, obeying the speed limit, his mother says, on some highway in Arkansas, when someone in a truck made a bad decision, pulled out in front of him, and that was it. Not even the full-face helmet he was wearing could save him.

I don't much like churches, but I've come to this one, a Catholic church in the hills of Pittsburgh, for my friend, to attend the funeral mass of her son. The truth is I don't mind churches of almost any faith but Catholic, because non-Catholic churches are a mystery to me, and I sort of like the mystery of unfamiliar churches and religions. They demand nothing of me, they remind me of nothing, they are often pleasant in the way that visiting a new park is pleasant. You look around at the people hanging out, at the playground equipment, the flowerbeds and trees, you walk around a bit, smile at the kid on a skateboard or a dog sniffing a bush, and then you go home. You have not been changed, nothing has been asked of you, no bad memories brought to light.

But I was raised Catholic, forced to attend Catholic school for nine years before I turned away from it for what still feels like forever. I know way too much about the Catholic Church to be able to relax in one as I might in, say, a Protestant church or a mosque or synagogue. I'm nervous, on guard, constantly waiting for something to go wrong. I know too much about the failings of the weak men who have sometimes sat as Popes, the equally weak men who have served as priests and preyed on young boys, too much about the failings of the Church dogma, especially in matters concerning women, too much about the witch trials of centuries past. I've been personally wounded by its failing to provide a meaningful spiritual compass for me as a child and young adult. Its rote questions and answers. Its stiff rites and sacraments. *Where do the souls of the brain dead go*, I asked a priest many years ago as my young brother lay in a coma from a drug overdose. He couldn't tell me.

I haven't been to a Mass in many years and I haven't taken Communion in maybe twenty-five years. While I do believe a man like Jesus may have lived a life not unlike the one that comes down to us in the New Testament, there's not a bone in my body I can force to believe in a God that allows such treachery and quackery to go on in his name.

Although of course every bone in my body wants to believe.

Sitting here in this church, near the front, hoping my friend can see that I'm here to support her, looking at all the trappings of that religion I've come to so distrust, the priests in their special funeral garb, the cross of the nailed Christ in the center, as horrifying as I remember from childhood, the statues of Mary and minor saints in the apses, all the candles lit, the altar with its Book of Gospels, the incense, the pews and the kneelers, I have wildly varying sensations: of disgust that rises like bile in my throat so thick I feel in any moment I will throw up, of great sadness for my friend, for her family, especially her daughter, who cannot stop sobbing, for the army men and women sharing this pew all stiff and mournful in their dress uniforms, men and women who were my friend's son's colleagues and friends. I can't stop crying myself, although I did not know the dead young man. His death reminds me of that of my young brother from a few years ago, and seems at the same time a foreshadowing of the one I fear for my own troubled son, this dead one's age, in the future. Sitting in the hard pew I feel myself literally present but also thrust back, sitting in a similar pew for the death of my brother seven years ago, and forward, sitting here for my beautiful son, who has been drinking himself into oblivion for many years now. Who will attend his funeral? Will I sit here alone, with no family, no god, no faith? I'm reminded of how my alcoholic father had alienated so many at the end that only a few family members came to his funeral.

I don't tend to like soldiers as a rule, but I like these, standing all tall and smart, wearing their medals and badges of honor, as my father, also a soldier, used to do at special occasions. My heart grieves for them, and for the rag tag motorcycle group, also here, with their long hair and polished motorcycles, standing brave and proud in chains and leather outside of the church, they, too, honoring one of their own.

The coffin is in the center aisle, draped with an American flag. I watch as the soldiers take the flag off and fold it carefully into a triangle to give to the dead one's mother, and listen as the priest says his words over the body of this soldier he did not know, and I wonder if these ceremonies can matter to any one at all except for those present.

I do not feel this space as a sacred space except for the fact that it contains a group of people who feel sacred to me, a community of women and men on a path to sobriety. My friend is one of these, and sprinkled among the mourners from the blood family, the army family, and the motorcycle family are us, members of that community.

I too am trying to live a life of sobriety. I'm trying not to fall into the death that my father and brother fell into, the one I fear my son seems also to be facing. Twice, he has called me in the last year to tell me he felt he would die if he didn't stop drinking, that he felt a death rattle, and more than once he has tried to stop but failed. I can only listen and take it in, I can only stop myself, I can't stop him.

I'm working on the third step, trying to give my life over to the care and will of a higher power, struggling to believe in a higher power that is not this God on the crucifix. I stare at the nails hammered into Jesus' hands and feet and wonder what it would feel like to hang from a cross.

We shouldn't mourn that my friend's son died like this, in an accident, the priest is saying, we shouldn't mourn that he didn't die an *honorable* death in a war; any death, he says, is an honorable death if the life one lived was honorable. I look at the ribs in Christ's torso, the crown of thorns, the look of resignation in his face. How can I give the care and will of my life up to this?

I've explored goddess religions, animism, even Voodoo and Candemblé. I have examined every kind of spiritualism that seemed to offer possibility of a belief in something larger than me, but either they have failed me or I have failed them, I cannot say which. This god hanging on the cross, the god that shaped my formative years, is only a reminder of how far I have come and how much I have failed to find what my new family calls a higher power.

When my friend finally walks up to the pulpit and has a chance to speak of her son I look at her face and try to force Christ out of my mind, although it's impossible to look to the front of the church and not see the Christ hanging on the cross. I force his image to recede in the background, and focus on my friend. She speaks of her son's life, telling some funny stories. She's strong and gentle and fair to everyone who is grieving, even her ex-husband, who sits, crumpled, in the front pew. She's a spiritual powerhouse, many years sober, and I want to be like her; I want her to be my higher power. I want to be able someday to stand in a church, like her, I don't want to be this trembling mess of fear that I sometimes am.

When I call my sponsor later to talk about the funeral, she reminds me that she and my friend have worked "the steps" many times for many years, for both themselves and those they sponsor, that it has taken work for them to get where they are, that I should stop beating myself up about it. I'm still young, two years old in that world and stumbling my way through the steps.

She, my sponsor, took me to a monastery a few weeks ago to talk me through the third step. I told her I was willing to turn my life over to a higher power but the truth is that I was willing but unable. I still feel stuck somehow, don't know what it means to have a caretaker that is not the God of the Old or New Testament.

Another of our tribe is here in the church singing. She has long dusty dreadlocks and is six months sober. She sings in a breathy, voice, heavy as honey, that reminds me a little of Sarah McLaughlan, "Then sings my soul, My Savior God, to Thee, How great Thou art! How great

Thou art!" she sings, "Then sings my soul, My Savior God, to Thee, How great Thou art! How great Thou art!" Over and over she sings the refrain, for what seems like a long time; there are stanzas that reference the beauty of the physical world as proof of God's greatness, the trees, the forests, the woods, the stars, the mountains, there is a stanza that focuses on the gift of God's son to us that leads once again to the refrain, "How great Thou art! How great Thou art!" and it hurts my soul to hear these words: can my singer friend really believe them, can my mourning friend, mother of the dead boy, really believe them? How can we be singing, on the day of such a death, *how great thou art?*

My friend is finished speaking, and the time for Communion has come. This is the moment, in the Catholic Mass, where one receives bread from the priest that is supposed to represent the body of Christ. It was always confusing to me, as a child, Communion. Was the bread a symbol or were we to believe it really was the body of Christ? It looked like a round, thin wafer, and none of the priest's chanting and incantations could change that. A wafer, not the body of God.

When I was younger we couldn't eat anything for three hours before Mass if we planned to have Communion, and we could not have Communion if we had any sins we had not confessed. The idea is that your body be clean both physically and spiritually, so that it seems like you are literally preparing to ingest the body of God.

Now everyone is lining up for Communion, and it crosses my mind that perhaps I should consider taking it. A wave of revulsion rushes through me—I don't want to commune with or have anything to do with this religion. But . . . I've said I'm giving my life to the care of a higher power, and wouldn't receiving Communion be a physical sign of that? My heart starts beating faster, and I can feel my knees trembling. Why am I here, I ask myself? What led me to enter this godforsaken church anyway? I look at the coffin, at my friend. I calm down. I see that my friend has taken Communion and is returning to her seat in the front pew. If I walk up to receive Communion I'll have to pass right by her. She'll see me. She'll know I'm here for her. I don't think she's seen me yet, since she arrived with her family and the coffin, and I've been hidden in the bowels of the church with all the other visitors. Maybe, I think, I should do this for her. I start my way down the pew, knowing that once I start there's no way to turn back. I keep going, although I'm frantically making an inventory of sins I might have committed in the last 25 years, since my last confession. I remember the face my mother used to make when my father took Communion during his once-a-year Christmas Mass, and I'm grateful she's not here to judge.

"He shouldn't be taking Communion," she would say, reminding the children that it was a mortal sin to miss Mass as much as he did, not saying what she must have known by then, that he was sleeping with other women, committing adultery. Still, who was she to know what was in his heart. Perhaps he became, for a moment, the altar boy he had been when he was younger, perhaps he felt, for a moment, the faith and hope he'd felt as a boy, and wanted to do something to honor it. Perhaps he had a momentary hope that taking Communion would help him to change his life.

I'm not unlike many others who want to have faith, who idolize those who have it, but who ourselves have little faith. We "refuse it even the smallest entry," as poet David Whyte writes in his poem "Faith." As I wait in line to take Communion I wonder if a small act like this, or some other small act, the writing of a small essay such as this one might open one to faith?

I don't feel anything when I take the communion wafer from the priest and put it in my mouth. I catch my friend's eye and she acknowledges seeing me, but I don't suddenly feel communed with God or filled with the Spirit. Truth be told I feel a bit like a fraud. The wafer tastes exactly like it did 25 years ago, tasteless and sticky, as I've written elsewhere, like a stamp you'd licked that had gotten stuck in your mouth.

Still, I'm not unhappy that I took the walk. I'm glad I tried. The priest reads us something from Matthew, "whatsoever you do to the least of my people, that you do unto me." Trying to swallow the wafer as elegantly as possible, I think, not for the first time, that perhaps god is in us, in my friends sitting in this church, not out in some abstract heaven.

"Our father who art in heaven," the priest starts, and we all chime in, "hallowed be thy name." It's the prayer with which we end every meeting of my recovery group. We always stand in a circle and hold hands. I'm always happy saying this prayer with my group, although I don't believe in this god the father. I do believe in the people whose hands

I am holding, though. It's the most powerful moment of the meeting for me: I feel an incredible electricity in the room, a raw power in the hands I am holding. It's as if for that moment, I'm tuned to some kind of god radio station that's directly linked into whatever higher power it is for which I'm searching. And maybe that's just what I need to practice, tuning myself to some station, some frequency that channels what I feel in the rooms of those meetings.

"In the name of the Father, the Son and the Holy Spirit," the priest is saying. "Amen," everyone is saying. The coffin is being escorted out, men with bagpipes are playing "Amazing Grace," we are all crying. The family follows the coffin, my friend leaning on her daughter, and then we all fall in, the soldiers, the motorcyclists and the drunks, some of whom can find god's station even in darkness, others of us still fumbling to get the right reception.

Thinking about the God of Questions on Winter Solstice

—for Janet Morgan

He's the subject of a huge painting given to me by an artist friend, and he shines above the fireplace mantel, the warm heart of my house. I love most the large white ball he holds in front of him, the ball that hides his nakedness. The ball's almost as large as his torso, and I cannot tell if the white of the ball is painted or bare canvas, whether it's a moon, a sun, or a full round nothingness, pregnant with all that we do not know, but would ask.

Sometimes I think I see destruction in the ball he holds. Other times, especially this darkest of nights, there's a questioning stillness there, a calmness I've seldom known. And in that calmness, hope. Sometimes I think it's my face the god holds, three years sober, turning my hopeful, empty face to the familiar dark.

II

First Days

You're pouring out of yourself, sobbing your way through an airport, you're wet with grief. *Not dead,* you think, *not dead,* just disappeared, visiting some other place.

You're blind, deaf with this new thing, a raging fetus, a demon that is all-consuming, as if you don't exist anymore, only this throbbing grief-monster, which owns you.

Weeping. Retching. Heart-cracking.

There are things to do, and you do them: you make the service preparations, you write the obituary, you pick out clothes to wear to the service, you call family and friends, you write down what you will say at the service, but you cannot manage this thing, like a fast-growing cancer, taking over every space where once was language and breath.

Back Home

You sit in the dark living room, lit only by a small glittering tree. You look at your favorite ornaments, gifts from your mother. Little clear houses with fan blades inside that twirl and dance over the tree lights. When you were a child, they seemed so magical you couldn't stop looking at them. You know it's the heat makes them twirl, not him.

Still.

The Amaryllis Bud

opens slowly over the weeks after his death—it will be in full bloom come Christmas day. Grief doesn't come into one fully grown. It's slow, long-living, not like this potted amaryllis, a gift that will die soon after blooming. No, grief's roots go deep, tough enough to last a thousand years.

Fifty Miles

Yes, there are two paths you can go by, but in the long run
There's still time to change the road you're on.
—Led Zeppelin, "Stairway to Heaven"

In the early morning hours of December 9, 2014, a widespread river of fog descended over North Texas, surrounding the Dallas Fort Worth metropolis and lingering into the afternoon hours. Seen from above, the fog seemed to swirl into itself, clotted into what looked like an endless sea that flooded the area, so thick that only tops of the tallest buildings in the skyline pierced it. Dozens of flights were cancelled at DFW. A dense fog advisory was issued, and newscasters warned that driving conditions were dangerous. In fact, the fog was so impenetrable in the morning that visibility was calculated at zero, making it almost impossible to drive.

It was into this fog that my son, Gray, drove that morning, headed about fifty miles northwest of his apartment in Dallas to the small town of Decatur. He had called in sick that morning to his job, although he'd told his girlfriend, with whom he lived, that he was going to work. A drive that normally takes a little over an hour would have taken much longer that morning as he plowed through a fog as nasty as any he might have ever driven through in his life. I don't know if he would have listened to the traffic or weather advisories, or even paid attention to them if he did.

He was driving to Decatur to visit his friend Bryce, a fellow musician and former band mate with whom he still occasionally collaborated, and who was known in the local music scene for his woozy electronic dance beats. Gray had told me that he admired Bryce as a musician and composer, and I know he felt a deep connection with him through the electronic music they both loved and composed.

Bryce was also an admitted heroin addict, who seems to have made his living selling drugs. Gray, who had completed a thirty-day rehab nine months earlier, had been staying away from him since his release because Bryce had been his source for drugs. In February, at Bryce's house, he had nearly died from a binge of meth, heroin, and alcohol, at one point vomiting blood and becoming psychotic, attacking Bryce, and his girlfriend. He would later tell me he thought he was a character from the TV show *True Blood*. He thought he had killed me. The blood he had vomited, he thought, was my blood. He checked himself into rehab two days later.

~

After completing rehab, Gray sent Bryce a text saying he didn't want to see him again, that he wanted his life to go in a different direction now. During a visit that summer he had confided how scary Bryce had become, how he had deteriorated into a wraith-like creature he hardly recognized, that his music had suffered. I could see that it brought Gray no pleasure to say these things, that it hurt and confused him to see what had become of his friend. Bryce had become a pariah in the music community, partly because of his notorious drug use, and partly due to his selling and promoting the use of heroin, opiates, and methamphetamine. Gray's friends told me Bryce would text them constantly to let them know of new shipments of drugs he had, even if they were drugs they didn't want. Gray's girlfriend told me that even if all you wanted from Bryce was pot, he'd try to talk you into something else. And in the past, Gray had hardly ever been able to resist.

But after Gray got out of rehab this time, head shaved, shiny recovery medallion dangling on his keychain, he said he was committed to staying clean and sober. Life was difficult, though. He was unable to find a job for about seven or eight months. Too many petty crime arrests. An outstanding charge from 2013 for possession of a small amount of meth was still unresolved. No one wanted to hire him. He sent job application after job application out, and almost hit bottom when even Jack-in-the-Box wouldn't hire him. Finally, in September sometime, he called me in Pittsburgh, where I live, excited to report he had passed a drug test and would be beginning work for Amazon, a seasonal job fulfilling orders through the end of the holiday season.

The decision to drive to Bryce's on that December day is a mystery. He had seemed to like his job and had made some good friends already there. Old friends and his girlfriend insist he seemed free of drugs, although he had started drinking again. His decision is like a fog of epic proportion that does not reveal a path, though you shine your brightest lights into it. Indeed, all your powers of analysis simply seem to obscure the matter. That's the mystery of fog, as anyone who's attempted to drive in it knows, that it does not respond as darkness does to light, by opening up a way, but rather just reveals more of itself. The powers of light are not useful in fog. The best thing to do is usually to wait it out, although few of us will do so if something we really want requires us to drive through fog to get it.

And yet, while I don't know what my son's reasons might have been, if he had them, to risk his life by driving in dangerous weather conditions to see a person who had become deadly for him, I can empathize. Thirty-five years earlier, when I was just a few years younger than Gray was that December 9th, I fell in with a skinny, dark-haired musician with a handlebar mustache. I was a junior at Southeastern Louisiana University in Hammond, and Fred had just graduated with a BA in music. He was the coolest person I'd ever met. We both played guitar, and he taught me some unique guitar tunings and turned me on to some wildly awesome Brazilian music. He liked Joni Mitchell's music, and impressed me with his knowledge of music in general. His collection of records rivaled mine in taste and breadth. At that time in my life the things I was proudest of were my music collection and the few small songs I'd written. Almost everything else was gravy. To my soul, only music mattered.

Fred and I met at a restaurant in Hammond where I used to tend bar. We hung out one night playing guitar and talking about music, and when he suggested we do some lines of coke I said yes. It turned out he knew as much about drugs as he did about music. We stayed up those first few nights drinking Scotch and snorting coke, and eventually making love. Over the weeks, he gradually worked up to asking me to shoot him up, showing me how to prepare a shot, then asked if I wanted to try. And because I trusted him—he was so cool, he knew so much about music and how to do drugs safely (clean needle, never share, he'd said), I decided to try it. And so we spent a summer shooting up coke and drinking Scotch, talking about music, sharing records, songs, playing guitar, and making love.

I became so bonded with him through the ritual of shooting dope and playing music that I would have done anything for him. When he said he'd be happier if I lost some weight, I did, I lost ten pounds in about three weeks. When he asked if I knew anyone who wanted to buy some coke, I checked around. We sold some to my brother, who would wind up dying a few years later of a drug overdose.

No one else knew this side of me. To almost everyone else, I was a third-year English major in good standing at Southeastern, a Joni Mitchell wannabe whose hobby was music. I did have clarity about wanting to finish college, but with respect to anything related to Fred, my mind was a haze. I couldn't see clearly what was happening to me, even though co-workers who spied the pin-prick bruises on my arms expressed concern, which I brushed off, in the way I imagine Gray would have brushed away the fog warnings. I knew what I was doing. I could handle it.

So, I get it, in a way. I get why Gray might have wanted to drive through the thickest fog ever to see the darkest friend ever who knew things about him no one else did. To see a friend, to whom he wouldn't have to lie. Fifty miles of fog. Did he ever think of turning back?

At some point, after a period I no longer remember, Fred broke up with me abruptly for another woman. From one day to the next I found myself abandoned, depressed, and feeling a hopelessness I had never felt before. Hammond was a small town; I had already seen Fred in a couple of our favorite restaurants with the new woman, which stabbed at both my heart and pride. What to do? It felt like some huge action had to be taken. Some purging thing. But what?

I had a friend in Baton Rouge who'd come through a tough time on drugs and would know something about what I was feeling. I decided I'd quit my job, leave Hammond, and move to Baton Rouge with her where we could share an apartment. It was only 50 miles away; I could commute to Hammond on Tuesdays and Thursdays to finish up my classes. I was as low as a person could be, my thoughts as clouded and black as they have ever been, but something in me chose life that day. If addiction is a river, I was still swimming in it, but I made a move to the shoreline that day instead of into deeper, more uncertain currents.

That 50-mile trip for me was all about choosing life, although I don't know that I understood it at the time, and I was lucky to have a friend who took me in. My choice will ever be a mystery, though, because I could just as easily have gone the other way; everything in my genes was screaming for that other way. Father, brother, aunt, all fallen to alcohol or drugs, others of the family on the way. Why I didn't follow them I'll never know. If I were a religious person, I would say something blessed me that day. But I'm not a religious person. Perhaps some part of me believed, as I still do, in the capacity for humans, even one as unworthy as I, to change, and the tiniest hope of change was enough to shove me just the tiniest bit that one day in a different direction. But I'm making this up. The truth is, I don't know why I chose life.

I don't remember what the weather was like when I drove the fifty miles from Hammond to Baton Rouge, that day 35 years ago, but I know I drove through a mist of pain and tears. And for months afterwards I rarely spoke except when it was necessary. I wore all black; I even wore a black beret. It was as if something or someone had died, and I was in mourning. I drank coffee with cinnamon and listened to the Keith Jarret's Köln Concerts over and over. I wrote horrible, sad poems, and played even sadder songs on the guitar. I found a job at a jazz bar in Baton Rouge. I commuted to Hammond on Tuesdays and Thursdays and plodded through my coursework. And slowly, slowly, I materialized back into a world without Fred, without drugs.

Who knows what was in Gray's heart as he drove his fifty miles to Decatur that day. Perhaps he was driving through a fog of pain and suffering that made the literal fog seem like clarity. Perhaps he was so out of tune with the moment, with the actual world, that he hardly noticed the fog, or registered it only as an irritation. Or maybe it echoed with some fog inside of him, some place he could never get clarity on, no matter how much he tried, no matter what light he shone on it. He had taken two packs of syringes with him, stolen from his girlfriend, who is a diabetic. She thinks he planned to trade or sell them to lower the cost of whatever drugs he was looking to buy.

The 911 call was made by Bryce from Gray's phone at 3:00 p.m. that day. Gray wasn't breathing. The paramedics managed to get a pulse, but were unable to stabilize it, and he was pronounced dead shortly thereafter. The detective who handled the case said Bryce's house was clearly a drug house. It was filthy, with needles and empty beer cans everywhere. The detective also said the only mark on Gray was a needle mark on his right hand.

Philosopher and former heroin addict William Pryor writes that "addiction is a philosophical mystery, more like that of, say, happiness. Neurochemists imagine happiness can be reduced to a chemical; most of us know it is far more elusive, the proper subject of mysticism, philosophy, psychology, literature, film, music and art." I don't want to give up on trying to come to some kind of clarity or serenity about my son's choices and my own, but I'm not certain I will come to the end of my life saying that I understand any of it. I feel compassion for his suffering, and empathy for his choices, though I wish every moment of every day he had not chosen to get up that morning and drive into that fog.

I sometimes wonder what would have happened if Fred hadn't broken up with me, if we had continued shooting up coke the way we were then. I was already doing whatever he asked of me, and had even stooped to selling drugs to my own brother. What else might I have done, or become, if he'd kept me around? Would I have chosen life if I had fallen so far into the river that I couldn't even see what life could be outside of it? Would I have driven fifty miles in a deadly fog to talk music, do drugs, have sex with him one more time if he'd asked me?

The fog is in us and surrounds us, insidious, seductive, suicidal. A cloud-river, coiled, coked, cooked, shot, knotted into itself so deep you can't see your way out. Some of us, through happenstance, stumble to the shore, others, their sights set on some prize the living do not perceive, lose sight of it.

Undoing a Death

Let's cheat, and start with the seconds before you stop breathing. First, move the needle away from the vein of your right hand. Don't let it touch the skin. Next, let it drop to the floor. Walk back to the living room where your drug-pusher friend is eating a sandwich. Leave him there. Do not speak to him, do not buy anything from him. Notice how filthy his house is. Tell yourself you do not want to die in a place like this.

Get in your truck and drive back to your apartment. Listen to NPR, your favorite radio station, on the way home. When you get home don't spend the morning rifling through your girlfriend's meds. If you don't search you won't find the benzos you think will complement whatever else you might do. Don't stash two packs of her syringes—she is a diabetic and needs them—into your backpack.

Don't call in sick to work at 7:15 a.m. You're not sick. You just don't feel like working. Kiss your girlfriend goodbye at 6:45 a.m. and drive to work.

It's crucial that you do not call your drug-pusher friend at 2:17 in the morning and arrange to drive out there later in the day (you are going to work, you are not going to drive fifty miles to the small town where he lives). Remember how scary you said he had become, how thin and wasted.

If you can't sleep, try reading or listening to music or just rolling over closer to your girlfriend. Maybe you can make love, or just hold her. Dream of the music you'll write, the children you'll have, the gorgeous mellowing that will come as you grow older. Close your eyes. Sleep.

Do not get up.

Essay in Search of a Poem

You've been trying to finish a poem for what seems like a long time. It's a poem that has to do with the death of your son. At first you can only manage fragments: images, lists, incomplete sentences. They are all good, strong words and phrases, stalwart witnesses to a struggling, fractured life, but they don't want to cohere into a poem. You have the bricks but not the mortar, the testimony but not the conviction.

It's painful to sit with it for more than hour at a time, to feel how impossible it is, even with poetry, to say any honest thing about your son's death that also honors him. To use the word *addict* in the old way that also means *devotion, consecration,* to look at his efforts at composing music, to see how he walked through the world with almost no skin, to say the hard truth but to resist the final labeling, the formulation of him sprawling on a pin, defined always by his last mistake.

You know poetry is the best way to say two things at once, so you keep trying. You do what you always do when you want to birth a poem: you scribble drafts in your special hand-made paper journal, you prop yourself up in bed, laptop on a pillow, trying to channel the wisdom of the body at rest; or you retreat to the third-floor room where the special table with the special wood from the special swamp in Louisiana waits, the wood with an eye, a wound in it, and you try to channel the wound and the friend who rescued the wood from a fallen cypress, a rescuing you could never accomplish with your son.

At some point, you finally have a draft of something like a poem, but you can see it's not working. It's rushing headlong toward some kind of false epiphany without earning it, it wants the high without the work, or maybe that's what *you* want, the rush to insight, the rush to closure, so you move stanzas around, add words and remove them, tweak line breaks, you even try right-margin justifying in the hope that this juggling will shock the poem to life.

You work like this for months because at some point you realize you've fallen in love with this poem, and you know you just have to find the right words, the right shape, to bring it into the fullness of being. You're starting to treat the poem as if it were your child, catering to its moods, taking the pulse of its strengths and nurturing those; but the revising goes on for so long with no real improvement that some days you feel nothing but anger at the poem and yourself. You lash out at it; ruthless, you slash lines, cut whole stanzas, crumple pages. You wish for a whip to beat the poem into submission.

And yet, you understand the poem's recalcitrance on some level. You know a poem grows a mind of its own that you must learn to recognize and follow; that's part of the mystery and wonder of poetry that you love, but *this* poem, *this* poem feels so important; you wrote the first words, you nurtured it, why doesn't it want to thrive?

You try bringing the poem to another country, thinking the new perspective will help you finish it, hoping the poem will like the fresh air, the different sites, the broader horizon. You bring it to coffee shops, you rewrite it by hand with beautiful fountain pens, and deep, sky-blue inks, you sleep with it on the floor next to you at night in case something comes to you.

But it continues to torture you in its unfinishedness, its spirit stubborn and relentless. You can't bear to let it go into that mass graveyard of unfinished, untitled and abandoned things, though, not yet, not *this* poem, you just need to give it a little more time, you just need to get a little distance, let the poem breathe on its own for a bit, then come back to it. Still, it's hard to leave it alone. You wake in the middle of the night to scratch out more revisions, and in the morning your husband asks if you had trouble sleeping. *Just a poem*, you say. He asks what it's about. *I can't talk about it*, you say, as if there's some terrible secret between you and the unfinished poem.

You begin to have nightmares about the imagery in the poem: the empty pill bottle and recovery chip on your son's keychain when they found him; how witnesses said his face had turned blue—but what *shade* of blue—in the moments before death, the sculpted beauty of his face— like Adonis—when you saw him afterwards. His lips, his eyes, closed. The needle puncture in his right hand. The half-written songs scattered on his computer. The rehab workbook with his crabbed handwriting throughout, the sharp truths of a life hidden from you.

You think of how your son referred to one of the last songs he wrote as less a song than a compilation of beats, and you wonder if he felt, in writing this piece you've listened to a hundred times since his death, its melody trapped in beautiful claustrophobic loops of phrases that fail to resolve, as you feel now, caught inside a cycle of words and lines that gesture toward a poem, but never grow into it.

And you wonder if maybe you've actually written all that can be written for now, a failed poem and the story of a failed poem, a eulogy and commemoration of everything that resists, fiercely, our efforts at closure.

Waiting for the Toxicology Report

Does it matter, to know what, exactly, caused you to stop breathing? The precise amount of whatever deadly thing you put into your body?

To get a meticulous survey: whether there are needle scars in your hand or in the crook of your arm, whether your liver is healthy or cirrhotic, how much your heart and brain weigh, how unremarkable your genitals, kidneys, your lungs? We think we want something literal, something we can know for certain, which some of us mistake for the truth.

January 9, 2015, 3:18 a.m.

You're dead a month today. Tonight one of your songs comes to me in a dream, you know, the one you called "weekend beats slow," the one you said was less a song than a collection of beats? Over and over it runs through my head, insistent, until it wakes me, and I can't help but feel you are trying to speak.

If you do come, I guess it will be in ways that are not embodied as you were on earth. I'm selfish, though, and want you back as you were, as a suffering, beautiful young man. But thanks for the music, if it was you.

And if it was some vision I created somehow from the bowels of the unconscious, some hallucination, well, *bring it on.*

Visitations

1

As dream you enter me: zombie-like, your eyes gone. *We cannot talk*, I say, *you're dead.* I wake, sick. This is not what I wanted, just another version of the nightmares I've had for years of you lost, stolen, flattened, stabbed, beheaded, gone.

2

I'm making puttanesca for the first time since you died. The scent of garlic and anchovies simmering in olive oil barely registers, the tomatoes, the crushed peppers, the sauce bubbling away, a sauce we both loved. It's the one dish whose recipe you asked for, the one you taught your girlfriend to cook. *He was always so worried about the garlic*, she said at your service, *that he would sauté it too long, and it would brown and taste funny.* I cut up black olives, chop parsley, grate cheese, spoon out a heap of capers to add to the sauce. The pasta water is boiling. I'm thinking of nothing but the next step in the construction of the dish, but as I stir the sauce, and the aroma envelopes me more intensely, I feel something like you for the first time since you died. It's like you're physically right next to me. I'm not expecting it, so at first, I don't pay close attention.

 Mom, you say, *I'm sorry.*

 I pour the penne into the boiling water.

 I'm sorry, you say again, though it's less a saying than a breath of something that's entering the edge of my consciousness. I ignore you, because you can't be speaking. You're dead. I give the pasta a quick stir before turning down the heat.

Again, more insistent, *I'm sorry, sorry*.

I'm stirring the pasta, but starting to feel your presence. Now you're pushing yourself into me, *notice me,* you seem to be saying, but it's hard to concentrate on noticing something I don't know how to acknowledge. I'm still too full of your death to hear, too focused on the food I'm cooking— yes, it's a recipe you loved, but I also remember you vomiting it up during the night once, me having to clean it up, your T-shirt, the bed sheets, your shoes, the carpet. I'm remembering how years later you told me you'd searched the house for alcohol that night, drank everything you found after I'd gone to bed. You must have been eighteen. I love you, I miss you, but I'm so angry with you.

I'm sorry, I'm sorry the presence, the ghost, the thing that is you and not you says and does not say, so pressing, so urgent I have to say, finally, despite myself, out loud, to the puttanesca-scented air, *I hear you.*

Ode to a Sea Star

Washed upon the beach, it's missing one full arm and half of another. I almost don't see it because it's the color of sand, light gray with darker gray specks. *Luidia Clathrata:* Gray Sea Star.

It's a smallish sea star, maybe slightly larger than my outstretched hand. It died young, surely did not reach thirty-five, the average lifespan of sea stars in the wild. Its body is covered with small scales. They look like rows of tiny gray corn kernels. I wonder if this one lost its arms to a shark, or maybe a ray, or even a gull. Sea stars can famously regenerate lost arms. They will sometimes purposely give up an arm to facilitate an escape.

Not long before he died I gave Gray a hand-painted Oaxacan wood carving of Pegasus, the flying horse who was Medusa's son. Pegasus was beloved of the muses, and I meant the gift to bring him luck in his work as a musician. When he left my house, he forgot to take the horse with him, and not long after it fell from its perch on a bookcase. Both of its wings broke off. I was worried that it was a sign of something bad, and tried to glue the wings back on. One stayed, but the other kept falling off. I finally gave up and kept it on the shelf with the broken wing next to it.

Some kinds of sea stars can regenerate an entire body from a lost arm, this because they're able to house most of their vital organs in their arms. I want to believe that something whole and new can come from a broken thing. I want to imagine the newly grown sea star crawling around on rocks and the bottom of the Gulf, happy, if sea stars can be said to be happy, eating clams and tiny fish, releasing its eggs into the ocean, pulsing salt through its arms until it finally dies, let's say in thirty years, of old age.

Morning Walk on the Beach

—for Maggie

It's early out, barely light. Sand sings between your toes with each wave of water, still warm from yesterday's sun. A man, half naked, is fishing. His skin looks burned.

A heron watches, its feathers slate-blue, the color of ocean. Egrets mill round like patients waiting for a doctor—they must be hoping the man will fumble his fish. Ahead, tracks emerge from the water, a trail of alternating commas etched into shore. You turn and follow them up to a dome of disturbed sand. Here's where the turtle stopped to dig a nest and lay her eggs. And here, the tracks show, she turned around to lumber back to sea.

Humans bury the dead to safeguard their bodies, or so we say. Turtles bury to shelter the small ones, letting sun and sand—not mother's body—warm them to life. You trudge on to an older nest, close to hatching. It's up higher on the beach, near sea grapes heavy with clusters of fruit, in the speckled shade of sea oats with fattening seed heads.

Before you reach the nest you see them, different tracks, oblong, the front paw prints larger than the back. Coyote. Then the deep hole that once was nest, unearthed, eggs sucked clean, shells scattered all around. So many broken ones you can't count. The white sand blinds you. Maybe this is why we bury our dead, you think, we don't want to see this. You shade your eyes and stutter down to the shoreline. So greedy, why is death so greedy? You walk away from the rising sun, feeling angry, you don't quite know at what.

This is nature, right? Kill or be killed. You press the weight of your body into the wet sand, watch your own tracks disappear as soon as you make them.

Visiting the Netherlands

So these farmlands are your stepfather's home, and I wanted you to know them, but did I really think these cows with their sad faces could diminish your despair? What could sheep and geese and ducks do for your pain? How useless, now that I know you'll be dead soon, to have strolled along the dikes, noted the birds and animals, patrolled the coasts of seas the Dutch manage so well, remarked on how well the streets are swept, the houses so neat and wide-windowed, framed with lacy curtains that let in too much light.

Maybe I hoped you'd find something useful in how your new relatives have learned to live with water, maybe I hoped you might be drawn to the crisp, painterly light here.

I see now that the landscape was too flat, too open, the sky too wide, the animals too domestic for someone who loves secrets as much as you. There's nowhere to hide, night the only refuge for the riddles of your hands.

You'd have preferred something rougher: Moors, a brooding sky. Wolves.

The Past

You're hiking a small path around a mountain lake. It's afternoon, the sun warm, the wind cool, the waters of the lake gray and still. It is one of those rare days when the full glory of the physical world reveals itself, as if a beloved were suddenly uncovering some new part of her body at each turn. You're surrounded by meadows dotted with hundreds of wildflowers of every color—cowslips and violets, thistles and clover, poppy and mallow, forget-me-nots, wild carrot and sweet-pea, sturdy tall grasses that ripple hundreds of shades of green in the wind. Further back are mountains of pine and chestnut as far as you can see.

You should be happy, but you also see the back of your husband farther ahead. He's angry with you. You've argued about some small thing, and as you look out at the lake, the meadows, the mountains, and the back of your husband, you think, for no reason at all, of how once you reach a certain age you can never go back and right anything. You can never go back to the moment your son was born and decide to raise him differently, for example; you can never go back to a moment when you chose one path over another, a path you now regret, or enter again into an argument where you uttered words that killed something somewhere. Not that you could ever have gone back even before you reached this certain age, but somehow you feel it more here, walking this lake surrounded by meadows and mountains. It's as if the impossible beauty of this place awakens its opposite in you, the ugly and more-than-possible past.

Or maybe it's just that the world around at this moment is so vibrant, so present, so much *what it is* and nothing else, that suddenly you feel it, too: that the past is what it is, and right now you are a woman with the husband walking away from her, a woman with regrets as large as these mountains, as varied as these flowering meadows you cannot change.

Into the Jungle

I fall into shadow, the midst
of things broken down,
and I look at spiders, and graze forests of secret inconclusive wood,
and I pass among damp uprooted fibers
to the live heart of matter and silence.
　　　　　—Pablo Neruda, "Entrance into Wood," tr. John Felstiner

You're on a boat riding that mother of rivers, the Amazon. A small boat, it's crammed with twelve of you, and it strains with the weight. The boat's strong but old, made of aluminum, lined with wood. It leaks a bit, water sloshes around in its bottom, and patches of something that looks like tar decorate its floor. The paint's chipped, and the boat's sides have small gouges in them. A wounded boat, one that still performs despite it all. You like the boat because it reminds you of what it's like to move through the world as an older woman. You're 61, and though you're in good health, your body has sprung a few leaks too. Your eyes and ears no longer work as they did when you were younger, your muscles complain a bit louder when asked to do to something new, and all wounds take longer to heal. Still you're here, passionate as ever in your role as teacher, bringing eleven students to the Peruvian jungle.

The air's heavy, filled with the moisture of a rain that has yet to come. Despite your passion for this place and what it has to teach your students, you feel heavy too. You wonder if the boatman feels that extra weight of grief, the weight that grows with every breath.

"Why did you have to go to South America, mom, when I was only eight?" your son asked, a full twenty years after that first visit to a jungle. You don't remember how you answered. Now, he's dead, and that question rises in you each morning, like a welt. Why then, why now?

That first trip was twenty-three years ago. You didn't yet have your first full-time teaching job. You were terribly excited: you'd never been to South America, and had been preparing for a year, studying Spanish. You wanted to write poems about the trip, you even secured a grant to support you while you were travelling. You wrote in your journal that the trip was a search for "God, a search for the sacred. A search for something LARGE." You wanted to go into the jungle, you wrote, because you wanted to be "where I didn't know the names/of things to learn them/as blood learns the way of veins."[2]

After some time, the Amazon narrows, and the boatman turns off onto a smaller tributary, the Tahuayo. You can see either shore much clearer now, can feel more intensely how sharply and often the river twists and writhes. It's the wet season, and much of the jungle is flooded, paths obscured, the only means of getting anywhere a boat. You can see up close the nuanced and oppressive greens of the jungle, a dense network of trees and vines, hanging aerial roots and epiphytes that feel comforting in ways you do not fully comprehend. You want it all to enter you, you want to hold its familiar strangeness against your heart like a balm. Maybe, you think, you still seek something sacred, something huge.

You feel the need to let the jungle know your son has died, even though you know this feeling is irrational. *I'm not the same*, you want to say, not the same as the young mother, adventure in her heart, who came to explore for a month when her son was young, not the same, even, as the middle-aged teacher who returned years later with students, to introduce them to its wildness. You're here now, once again, with students, and you don't know, exactly, how you're different, except for being older and grief-stricken, but it seems important to announce this death to a place you've come to love.

You hear the *keer* of a hawk before you see it, floating in the sky, the chatter of parakeets as they break into flight, looking like explosions of colored petals speeding through air. You're deaf in one ear, but you can still hear the *whowho* of the plumbeous pigeon and the shriek of the screaming piha, half wolf-whistle, half warning. Over the next hours the boat moves closer toward your new home, a lodge in the flooded jungle, and you bask

---

[2] "Why I Went Into the Jungle," *How Heavy the Breath of God*. Denton: University of North Texas Press, 1994.

in the kaleidoscope of birds crisscrossing the river: Boat-billed herons, Amazon kingfishers, Yellow-billed terns, Neotropic cormorants. Turkey and yellow-headed vultures sit in groups at the tops of trees, unmoving and unmoved at the noise of the boat's motor. There's more diversity of birds in this small area than in the entirety of North America, and there's something about the vibrancy of all that difference that fills you with hope.

The birds don't care that you've returned, and they don't care that you're bringing students again. The birds don't care that you hope something of the jungle gets its claws into these young ones. And yet. Somehow you feel welcomed, as if the birds represent some spirit of this part of the world that recognizes you as sister, daughter, yes, maybe even lover.

The river is the color of deep green tea. It's also, you think, the color of continuing. The river never gives up. Even in the dry season, the guide tells you, there's a channel of water here.

The breeze feels good as the boat makes it way down river. You have the sense of moving through the artery of some unseen beast, an artery pulsing with river-blood, a rush of something that will not be denied: It's too late to turn back. And what would be there if you turned back? The death of your son, the one who will never return. The only thing to do, the river seems to say, is to move forward. The river, the birds, the trees and the animals the trees are harboring—monkeys, sloths, snakes, frogs, bats—they don't care about your grief. Maybe that's part of what draws you back here, to this place of intimacy with nature. The denizens of this jungle will not try to be compassionate, will not ask you to tell about your grief. Like the river, their only song is a song about continuing.

After several hours the river narrows again, and you arrive at the lodge, which consists of a series of thatched-roof building perched on stilts high above water. You'll stay here for many days in a simple screened room. You'll sleep breathing Amazon air, sweet and yeasty, spending mornings and nights on small boats and canoes looking for birds and animals. Just looking, nothing else. You'll sink into the rhythm of heat and shade, rain and sun, the few modalities of the jungle. It's good, you think, not to have many choices. It's good to just look and listen for a time.

You can hear the water lapping at the stilts underneath your room, and you feel protected: the ceilings of the rooms are covered with nets to prevent the boas that sometimes nest in the rafters from slinking down. You'll see boas and tarantulas in other parts of the lodge, but never in your room, and you'll sleep with mosquito netting draped around your bed at night.

Crack of dawn, the morning after you arrive. You slather on insect repellent and sunscreen, binoculars in hand for a boat ride to look for birds. You'll do this each morning with Andy, one of your guides, and one or two other early risers, including Kenny, a dark-haired student a little younger than your son was when he died, who joins you every morning. On these morning rides, you'll see more kinds of herons and kingfishers than you knew existed, cormorants, hawks, macaws and parrots, caciques, and a rare umbrella bird; you'll see a toucan and a fruit crow. You'll see anis and seedeaters, kiskadees, tanagers and hummingbirds, the squirrel cuckoo. All this amidst a wash of jungle color that looks like an impressionist painting: lime greens and olive greens, black greens and brown greens, the startling white bark of dead trees. Bird songs and clatterings, grunts and cooing, jeets, raspings, growls and mellow whistles. But nowhere the voice of your son. Or, maybe, everywhere the voice of your son. You remind yourself that you spread his ashes last year in the waters of a creek in Texas. Could it be, you wonder, that part of the sand of his bones has entered these waters? Could it be that his spirit lives, along with all those others we have lost, here, in sky and water, fish and bird and animal?

Late morning, after breakfast, a second boat ride, looking for mammals this time. Your guide, Javier, points to a dark shape in a tree on the nearest shore. The boat slows and inches to the edge.

"A sloth," he whispers, "three-toed sloth."

At first, it's hard to distinguish the body in the top branches of the tree from the tree itself, but finally you see it, moving slowly, one huge shaggy clawed arm, then another, the giant triple claws extending from the arm. Sloths are so sedentary that algae grow on their coats, giving them a greenish tint and helping them blend in with the trees where they spend most of their lives.

"This one's a mother," Javier, says, "see the baby with her." You don't want to see a mother with a baby, so you look away. You who have no baby, no child any longer. You feel ridiculous, selfish, but still, you look away.

You're with the same three guides throughout your visit, and you come to trust them. Andy is good with birds. Javier is excellent at finding mammals, Claudio is best at finding poison dart frogs, and is also perhaps the strongest of the three. Together, they know so much; you wish you had a guide like one of them for matters of the heart.

"This is why young people die of heroin," the guide would say, and "this is how we can prevent it."

"Here are the endangered young men," the guide would say, and "here is what we must do to save them."

You'll see monkeys on many of these boat trips over the next week: Pygmy marmosets with tails longer than their bodies, Saki monkeys with furry-hooded faces, strapping wooly monkeys and pink-faced rhesus monkeys, but with rare exceptions these sightings are often just glimpses, as the monkeys don't really want to be seen. Even when the group is quiet, and in a quiet boat, the monkeys will move quickly to hide behind a clump of leaves or a large tree limb. The most you get is a flash of something moving, leaves shaking, a quick tail or face. It can be frustrating, trying so hard to see something, your eyes laser-focused, the guides on the lookout, the sun hot, the trip long, to see just a flash of something for an instant. It's perhaps easier on you than on the students, as you're older, and it's not the first time you're peering into a jungle. You've had more time to learn patience, or at least pretend you have. The jungle doesn't give up her children lightly, though, no matter how deep the looking. So much staying power needed for this seeing and hearing. It's not unlike what you need for a poem, you think, or for an insight that might find its way to an essay.

Despite the difficulty of seeing in a place where flora and fauna have evolved for camouflage, you will see many small creatures: bullet ants and jumping spiders, the yellow-crowned brush-tailed tree rat, a small hummingbird nest with two of the tiniest chicks you have ever seen; an Amazon tree frog with huge eyes, a tiny caiman.

And you'll have more experiences with larger mammals. On a boat trip farther out on another day you're rewarded with a more intimate encounter with fat wooly monkeys. You get so close to them you can see that their fur is chocolate and caramel-colored. They have curious faces and long, muscled arms that reach for the bananas you proffer.

"They know when the boat stops," Javier says, "that there will be bananas. That's why they're so friendly."

"These are rescued monkeys," he continues, "they're used to humans, even though they've been returned to the wild." He says they've been rescued from the "black market," which means those who sell them to Peruvian circuses and tourists, or others who wish to keep them as pets.

For just a few minutes you forget your heaviness as you reach, banana in hand, toward one of the saved ones. The monkey comes out to the very edge of a branch, stretches out his long arm, and grabs it. Your fingers almost touch, and you smile.

After the monkeys, Javier steers the boat down a different channel, where he points out another sloth feeding at the very top of a tall tree. He explains that sloths like the new shoots of the leaves. That's why you will so often see them in the crowns of trees.

"Males have bright orange spots on their backs. Females do not," he says. You ponder the value of these spots. For whom are they valuable? Do females need to see the spots to recognize any given sloth as male? It seems paradoxical that the males would sport such color, as they've evolved so well to avoid detection. But it's not unlike the male frigate bird's red throat pouch that he will inflate to attract a mate, making himself vulnerable to predators. Perhaps it's a sign of bravery to blatantly defy the need to camouflage; perhaps only the strongest dare to expose themselves in this way.

Sometimes you wish you had a mark on your back, the kind of tattoo many of your female students sport. Maybe your tattoo would say something like *My only child is dead.* A friend of yours made a beautiful quilt after her son died. One side is made of cloth the color of dusky lavender; on the other side's a plain white field with huge black lettering: *I am a woman whose child is dead.* Your friend said she wanted to express what it felt like to walk around after the loss of a child, to have to pretend on some level to be okay, but to have an agony unknown to others that you carry within.[3]

---

[3] Penny Gold, "Self-Portrait, Year 2." See http://whileshenaps.com/2016/05/i-am-a-woman-whose-child-is-dead-quilt.html

One day the group boats farther than usual, to terra firma, to find poison dart frogs, although Javier says we will also see a bat cave. The trail is so overgrown it's hard to recognize as a trail, but today Claudio is the lead guide, and he knows this forest like his knows his mother's face because he grew up here. He's vigorously macheting—and creating—the trail ahead. You stay close behind him, admiring the vitality of his young body, the sureness with which he cuts away vine and leaf to make a way for the group.

It's impossible to walk through a jungle like this without being touched by it both literally and figuratively. The path is narrow, spiny leaves stick into your skin as you pass, and lianas grab at your hair. You sense the thick web of a spider just as you walk through it. A tarantula stares at you, waiting on the side of a tree. You see it, but only seconds before you reach to put your hand on the tree for balance. Mud sucks at your boots, mosquitoes and other insects sip at your skin. You're hot and sticky but not unhappy: You're amazed at the intelligence of the jungle, walking palms that move their roots to find light, epiphytes whose seeds germinate in the tops of trees, creating aerial roots that grow down from those tree tops to reach soil, palms covered with spikes that protect them from animals (natives use the spikes to make poison darts). There are giant kapoks and many trees you cannot name, plants you cannot identify.

You do recognize the bromeliads, though, tucked into the arms of trees. The centers are filled with rain water and, sometimes, poison dart frogs live there with their young. You'll see four frogs on this hike: two red, and two golden. They are tiny, hardly as big as your thumbnail, and exquisitely colored: the golden frogs are bright yellow with black stripes and dots, while the others are lined with red, have a black and yellow stripe down the middle, and silver legs with black dots. You're amazed at how small and exquisite they are, like jewels.

Claudio coaxes one out of its bromeliad cup, and onto a leaf so that the group can see it. He lets the frog hop onto his hand while Andy explains that the poison is in the skin glands of the frogs, and why it will not kill Claudio (he would have to swallow it, he says). Claudio lets the frog hop back into its cup and rinses the skin the frog touched on his hand and arm.

Chemicals extracted from the skin of some poison dart frogs have been shown to have medicinal value. Scientists have attempted to use it to make a painkiller that's 200 times as potent as morphine. The therapeutic dose, however, is very close to the fatal dose. The image of your son with a needle in his wrist, shooting up heroin for the last time flashes through your head again. Even though he's been dead 18 months, there's not a day, not a night, that goes by that this image doesn't haunt you. You remember him admitting to you, the year before he died that he was a "self-medicating drunk and addict," and you wonder how many others misjudge how much of a substance will kill their pain, without killing them.

As the group begins the walk back to the boat, you notice how huge the trees are here. You cannot see the tops of many of them. One of these giants has fallen, and is partially blocking the path. Long-nosed bats are lined up along the outside of the tree, but the inside of the tree is completely hollowed out, Andy says, and there are also bats inside. This is the bat cave, he says, and asks who wants to go in. You don't even have to think, *of course*, you will enter it, even though you can't see where it ends. After a few moments Claudio stoops down to enter the tree, you follow him, and notice that Kenny, the student who's been birding with you each morning, is right behind you. You don't realize until you emerge from the cave that no one else joins you. The others will walk around the outside of the tree and meet you at the other opening.

It's exhilarating to crawl through this tree, the multitudes of bats awakening and flapping their wings, making a cool animal breeze against your face, the sweet, almost genital, smell of earth and wood. There's no stink, just the aroma of softly rotting wood. Your flashlight illuminates much larger bats hanging from the top of the hollow tree: a mix of fishing bats, whose faces resemble bull dogs, fruit bats who wrap themselves in their wings as if with a blanket, and much smaller vampire bats. You experience a rush of adrenalin. It almost feels as if you are hallucinating. You are entering wood, you are entering "the live heart of matter and silence," as Pablo Neruda writes.

You're crawling on hands and knees, but you don't mind. Are there termites? Guano? Maybe, but you don't look down, and only sense mud sucking at your boots. Kenny will tell you afterwards that he watched a thumb-sized cockroach crawl over your foot; he'll say there were *thousands* of bats. He'll see spiders and hundreds of insects, including mosquitos in the glow of his flashlight. You are not thinking of roaches or mosquitoes or numbers of bats. You are inside the heart of a tree, you are inside the home of those our culture has demonized. It's like the underworld here, you think, and you trust Claudio, who barely speaks your language, but knows the language of this jungle, to get you through.

The breeze from the bats' wings, a gray and brown blur, feels insanely lovely. In fact, you feel a bit crazy and lost, in a good way, inside of the tree. Kenny will remember more specific things: Bats streamed out of a hole in the tree's ceiling "like a column of black smoke," he'll write later. Kenny will also write that he was afraid to enter the tree cave, at first, that he worried about the bats being dirty and loud, infecting him with something while in the cave, about rabies, malaria. You had not thought about any of these things, so seductive was the open mouth of the tree, the entrance to the world of the other.

In an essay he writes for the class, Kenny will say that at a certain point something in him shifted while crawling through the cave, "One minute," he writes, "I was revolted by the squish of mud and guano beneath my boots, the nutty, fecund smell of decaying earth, the furiously beating leather wings that caressed the top of my head and neck; the next, being inside that tree felt perfectly natural. Now, the wildness of nature felt like the norm, while my resistance to it felt uptight."[4]

You smile when you read his essay weeks after the trip. Something of the wild snagged him during the crawl, and the teacher—mother— in you is grateful.

That night, after a cold shower, you survey your body. Insect bites on your ankles—a mix of mosquito, chigger, sand-fly and god knows what else—some of which are threatening to get infected. You slather cortisone on your legs. Scratches and bruises on your arms. Your back's aching from sitting upright in a boat with only a backless board seat for hours at a time, but you're still happy to be here, to have had the experience in the tree cave. You sleep deeply that night.

---

[4] Kenny Gould, "Creature Comforts," unpublished essay.

The next morning the group goes out early to fish for piranha. Javier takes you and five others in a small boat to a shallower area of the flooded forest, harder to navigate because of a plethora of tree roots and small tree trunks, which fish like because of the protection they offer. There's fast-flowing water rippling through the trunks and roots. Perfect habitat for piranha. Javier tells you that wild piranha have a bad rap. They're not the demons you see in film and on TV. It's true they'll go after sick and dying animals and other fish if it's the dry season and they're hungry, but you're here in the wet season. Not to worry, he says. You fish with simple tree limbs and line. The group catches many fish, including several red-bellied piranhas. You're amazed at how beautiful they are: the shock of red at the belly is the color of an intense summer sunset. The guides cook them up for dinner that night, lightly frying the whole fish, head and all. The meat reminds you a bit of halibut, deliciously light and sweet.

And so the days pass in the flooded jungle: mornings looking for birds, afternoons boating to see monkeys or sloths or whatever you can see. Nights looking for those, like your son, who are nocturnal: tree frogs, owls, caimans, spiders, bats. In between, food and naps on beds with mosquito netting, cold showers, lots of insect repellant. And then you get up and do it all again.

There are days, though, when you just want to have fun. One sunny day you spot pink river dolphins jumping in the water alongside the boat. Their frolicking is infectious. The guides anchor the boat in an oxbow lake and you all jump into the water. Some of the students worry about being attacked by piranha or anaconda or caiman, but they jump in anyway. The guides also swim, keeping us near the boat and away from the edges of the lake. The dolphins keep their distance and eventually leave, but you and the students float in the sweet and cool waters for much of the afternoon, the students splashing and joking. You've been with these students constantly for almost ten days by now, and they are beginning to feel like family. You've been known to say, tongue in cheek, that students are like children who listen to you (although that is not always the case). Your son once told you that he sometimes felt like he had a secret brother or sister because you'd talk to him so much about one student or another over the years. Certainly this group has bonded like a family. Several have shared and faced deep-seated fears—of insects, spiders, snakes, even of travel by water—on this trip. Only time will tell how much of a difference it will make in their lives back home, but you're hopeful, as you lie back on your float and watch them splash in the water. At the end of the day hope may be all you have. Maybe, you think, hope is best understood as a kind of prayer. Once, before your son died, you felt such a sense of hopelessness at the direction his life was taking, that you asked your therapist to tell you what you might do about it.

"Pray," he said, knowing you were not a person who prayed, "you can pray."

And so comes the day when you all load back into a boat, this one a bit newer, bigger, swifter than the one that brought you here, and head down the Amazon toward a plane that's waiting for you in Iquitos to take you back to North America. Your head is full of images and sounds from the hard looking and listening. You hope your students will discover how much this intense looking and listening is always the job of the writer, no matter how tame or wild the place you find yourself.

You look out at the river and trees as the boat takes you all away. You're thinking this flooded jungle is bursting with hope, you're thinking it's filled with millions of small prayers.

One Morning

You wake up and are surprised to find that for a few seconds you have not thought about your son.

Soon there are even some days where for a whole couple of minutes you think about something else exclusively: your work, a recipe, a letter or text you're writing to someone. You're beginning to remember that the world is filled with things other than his death. You don't want to realize this, at first. There's a part of you that wants to hold onto thinking about him, is afraid if you forget, if you don't remember everything, his life will have been meaningless. As if you are the only keeper of his memory.

After a while you begin to think that maybe you don't need to have quite so many photographs of him in almost every room of the house, from the time when he was a child to more recent times, a few months before his death. Pictures of the two of you laughing, hugging each other, looking like everything is fine. The photographs are beginning to bother you just a bit. They seem false, somehow, the smiles a pretense, at least the more recent ones, when he was so lost and you couldn't find a way to help. The photographs make you sad, but you can't bear, yet, to take even one down. Somehow that would seem a betrayal. But you're beginning to think that you don't need the photographs to remember him. He's burned into you.

You still feel cut open, and you've hardly smiled yet, nothing but a kind of sick turn of the lips to acknowledge a friend's condolences, or casserole, potted plant or gift of a candle. But a day comes when you actually make a broad smile, and sort of laugh when someone says something funny.

You had not thought anything could ever be funny again. You had not thought you would ever laugh, would never not mourn. But now, two years after his death, you can feel the wound tightening just a bit, the way the deep cut on your arm has been, the one made when you tripped down the stairs. For weeks your arm bled, even with bandages, at the slightest brush with anything, then finally scabbed over, though even the scab would chip and bleed if you weren't careful, and now when you look at it you think this is what your heart must look like, red and inflamed around a round center of dry blood, the tissue around it shiny and beginning to scar.

Hiking in Wyoming, After a Death

It's these ancestral mountains, massive as grief,
that dominate, sharp, angular,
     fragments
         jutting out like fingers or hands.

               Split, shattered, cracked,
                  ruptured,
          they bare fracture after fracture
       from the ancient wound that made them.

       ~

             It's summer, the sun fierce
            as a new mother, but snow
              still hugs the peaks,
          defiant as a young child,
                wanting,
               but refusing,
                to let go.

       ~

You make your way slowly up, around and over
      the mountain, sagebrush and pine scenting the air,
         mocking memories of other times—
            (winter holidays, children who still came home).

~

From the ridge, a rainbow of green in the basin—
        sage and silver green, moss green, gray-green, white-green, blue-green,
            grass-bright green, lime and sea green, mint, so many
         you think that green must surely be the color of grief, or god.

You reach down to twist a new shoot from a sagebrush,
its thin leaves a wash of pastel, silver,
water-colored.

You crush the leaves between your fingers,
breathe in deep

as you used to take in his scent at night,
that last kiss, the sweet smell of boy,
then the tucking in—

                      you wish green
           could be suckled like milk from breasts,
              or taken in one's mouth like air.

~

The whooshing of the creek, like a crowd applauding or cheering. From
here you can see it twining around the foot of the mountain—so noisy, so
much in a hurry, white water frothing up. Why is it so angry,

                  when will it still to pool?

~

                  A black snake's frozen

into a flat curl
in the middle of the trail.

You walk around it,
turn
to see a doe and her fawn.

They freeze, you freeze,
and in that moment

you catch the doe's eyes,
large and skittery.

You wonder what she would do
to protect her child,

then she bounds away,
the fawn following.

~

It's morning, but the sun acts like it's noon. The harsh light feels like poison entering your skin. Your mouth and throat dry with dust.

There's such a thing as too much light, of seeing too much, you think. You walk for an hour without shade, consider that you could die if you made a wrong turn, or your water ran out. The trails scattered already with the dried bones of trees.

Finally, a lone juniper tree. You stop, sit in its shade, grateful, take some water from your pack.

A magpie flies out of the tree in a black and white flash, cawing a song. The beginning of an old nursery rhyme runs through your head:

One for sorrow,
Two for mirth,
Three for a funeral . . .
And four for birth

Closing your eyes, you hope for another.

~

You keep walking in sun, wishing it away until finally it leaves, the wind comes up, you're climbing again, and it's almost cold enough for a coat. Vireos, robins, more magpies, a sky-blue bird that disappears almost as soon as you see it.

Another bird's singing a long song you wish you could understand. The song's so complex, it feels like sentences you should be able to make sense of, but you can't. A tiny brown bird flies right up to your face and stops, beating its wings with what almost seems like glee for a second, as if it wants to say something, then changes its mind and disappears.

Maybe joy is like that, you think, unexpected, mysterious, fleeting

~

Ticks hide in high grass
waiting for breath or body,
a shadow.

You'll find one on your skin later,
its head almost too deep inside you.

You'll pull her out, but you won't mind
that something from this place,
so generous with itself,

wanted something from you.

~

A jackrabbit crosses the trail,
stops, looks at you

before bounding away,
pink-skinned ears flaring.

~

The trail winds down until you're at a small stream buzzing with color. Gossamer-wing butterflies, pale blue, and white-yellow, flit over and around the water.

The pale blue ones—they're called Blue Melissa—are marked with dark dots on the underside of their wings, an orange row of spots along the edges. Their larvae feed on wild lupine, which must be where the wings get their color. Breathtaking treasures that will only live a few weeks. You know beauty cannot last, though you might wish it could. Better, you tell yourself for the hundredth time, to feel blessed to have encountered it at all. *The subject of the poem,* Galway writes, *is the thing which dies.*

~

You keep walking. It's all you know to do.

~

Breaking the skyline of a ridge,
            the headless scarecrow of a cedar tree,
                        its craggy trunk hollowed out by age or
some misery
only the eldest of us know.

        Its limbs stretch out, cross-like, emptied of leaves, as if
                        to bless or scare.

A marker, a reminder, as if you needed one,
that everything you see and touch and love will die.

Other cedars, stunted but still living, crouch nearby.
Knobby and twisted, their trunks whipped by wind,

roots embracing rock,
they've found a way to last longer.

~

You're trying not to see death everywhere.
You look to the sky, unbroken cornflower blue,
big as your love for him, which death does not diminish.

Concentrate on love, you tell yourself.

Nothing's hidden here, you say to no one at all,
        the sky makes all achingly bare.

~

At the end of the trail
        a rabbit sits in an opening
        in the rock, behemoth boulders
stacked above the opening.

You wonder if she can sense
how dangerous this hiding place is,
how heavy the boulders,

how, like regret and sorrow,
they could crush at any moment.

~

You turn back, and this time you look for flowers. They're everywhere: lupine and larkspur, wild iris, yarrow and primrose, phlox, wild geranium. Snow buttercup, beardtongue. Paintbrush, trailing daisy, dwarf sunflower. Wild chamomile.

Some, tiny and vibrant, have rooted in crevices of rocks. Like the butterflies, they'll not last long, but oh how they brighten with their small, mortal lights.

~

What to do with such a quarrelsome heart as yours, a heart that does not agree with Death, amid this stunning, indifferent landscape?

Give it away, something, maybe the wind, says—

Give it to the wild and brave flowers,
just passing through, like him.

Give it to the mountains, the scruffy trees,
the recalcitrant snow, the greedy ticks,

the birds and their ambiguous messages,
the sage, the glorious greens, the creek.

Give it to sun, savage as he was,
give it to the sky, uncluttered and sweeping,

give it to the mountains rising against it,
like you, broken,
resilient.

Memory, Ever Green

—for my father, Jules François St. Germain, 1930-1989

When they begin the beguine
It brings back the sound of music so tender
It brings back a night of tropical splendor
It brings back a memory ever green
      —Cole Porter, "Begin the Beguine"

I'm walking the streets of Paris at twilight, humming Cole Porter songs from a film I just watched at a local cinema. Artie Shaw's rendition of "Begin the Beguine" weaves its way into my head, and suddenly my father's there too. This was a song he loved, one he could play by ear on the piano.

Born in Louisiana to a Cajun mother, my father spoke French, but he'd never been to France. I walk Boulevard Saint Germain and imagine him walking with me. He would've made jokes about our last name appearing everywhere. We would've stopped to take a photo under the street sign of our name; maybe we would've lingered over a café at Les Deux Maggots while we looked out at the abbey of Saint-Germain-des-Prés. His would have been a *café noir*, with lots of sugar. He wouldn't have cared about the famous writers who once frequented the place, though he might have asked again why I chose writing for a career when marrying a rich doctor would've made for a more stable situation. He would've asked, as he always did, about my "love interests." Maybe, in a city so full of magnificent churches, he would've reminisced about his years as an altar boy.

He's not here, though, and the last time I saw him was in New Orleans, twenty-eight years ago. He was 59 then, dying of cirrhosis, his stomach swollen, his skin turned orange, several of his teeth missing. I hadn't seen him sober for many years, maybe twenty. He could barely talk before he sank into the coma from which he never awakened. He would die a few months later in a VA hospital.

This is the image that's dominated my memories of him for the last twenty-eight years, as grotesque and sick, an alcoholic who killed himself with drink. A year before my father died my son, who was four then, would say "Gramps looks like a monster," and ask if we could please not visit him anymore. I was afraid for my father as he neared what I suspected to be the end of his life, but I was also afraid for me, and for my son. I had a taste for drink as well, and worried I would, one day, become my father. My aunt and brother had already died young of substance abuse and I feared those genes were in my son's blood as well. We called it the family "curse."

The first thing I always say about my father, when people ask, is that he was an alcoholic and that he died of cirrhosis. I don't say he worked two jobs the entire time he and my mother were married to support five children, one of which was as a Command Sergeant Major for the National Guard. I don't say that he worked at his second job, as night manager of a bowling alley, up until the day he went into the hospital to die, that he was never fully able to take retirement. I don't say he was a good dancer, I don't say how funny he was, or how he liked children, I don't talk about how good he was at piano, I don't mention "Begin the Beguine." Since his death, in my mind he has been defined by the thing that killed him, the very thing I've been afraid, most of my adult life, that would kill me or my son.

But today I've been sober for seven and a half years, and I work with women who are in recovery. My son did become an alcoholic and addict, and like my father, never recovered. I'm stable for the moment, but there's never a day I don't think, even if just for a moment, about having a glass of wine. There's a part of me that blames my father—his model as well as his genes (though I'm aware it's not fair to blame someone's genes) for my own struggles and for my son's death.

Gray died two years ago, and since his death I've worked hard to understand what a complex person he was, such that my memory of him is not defined always by what killed him. I haven't always been successful, but it's seemed important to keep in mind his strengths as well as his weaknesses. Like my father, he loved music. He played piano and composed songs. He nurtured other musicians. He loved video games and computers. He was an addict and alcoholic, but he was also much more than that, something I remind myself every day.

Perhaps it's time to see my father through more compassionate eyes. The song he loved so much that's rumbling around my head today reminds me he was once a young man with hope and promise. My mother said he played the violin when he was young, and was very good at it. Something about these historic streets wakens other memories, too, some actual, some from photographs: I see him, a young and handsome dark-headed man, dancing with my mother, jitterbugging across a dance floor, I see him swirling her around, she laughing and beautiful, he seductive and confident. I see him smiling and naïve, proposing to her, I see him holding her close and dancing to Artie Shaw's big band music. I see him in their wedding photos at twenty-two, with his new short haircut, the wavy curl at the top, I see him smiling as he runs out of the church with my mother in a rain of rice. I see him at thirty with three children, at thirty-six with five. I see him working two jobs, leaving home early, coming home late, I see him on Sundays sitting at our piano playing "Begin the Beguine" over and over, his stubby fingers pounding away in a bumpy, staccato fashion, I see him picking up a Lucky Strike and taking a long drag between repetitions, my mother calling him to dinner once, twice in a sharp voice. I see him, Scotch-drunk and dancing with me at a carnival ball when I'm fourteen, sloppy now, and a surge of sadness fills my heart.

The sky darkens and rumbles. I feel drops of rain, duck into the nearest café and order a café au lait. I pull out my headphones, click through iTunes to find my own loved version of the song, Ella Fitzgerald's. Shaw's version is an instrumental; this one has lyrics. I press *play*, and listen, sipping my coffee and looking out at the rain falling, covering the city in a gray slick. I back it up, press *play* again, tears now falling freely as the rain. I'm glad to be in Paris for the summer, a city where no one seems to care if you're crying.

This song he loved, I'm just realizing, was about loss, about wanting to hold on to moments of joy you'll never know again. Maybe you've got to have lived through a great love that slowly disappoints over the years until it almost becomes either hatred or numbness, to enter the depths of this song's lyrics. I understand why he might have wanted to drink to find that feeling again.

I pay for my coffee and resume my walk, listening, now, to the Artie Shaw version. I walk across the Seine to Isle St. Louis, from there across the Seine again to Notre Dame then wind my way through the streets of the Quartier Latin and Boulevard St. Germain, then back up the river and along where the book stalls are, then across the Pont des Arts, wondering what my father would have thought of Paris. It's twilight now.

Moonlight spills onto the waters of the Seine under the Pont des Arts, the bridge with all the lovelocks on it, so many the grill's beginning to bend with the weight of them. It's a stunning view, the bridge a clichéd romantic spot in the middle of a romantic river and city. Of course, the young would come here to etch their names on padlocks then throw the keys in the water, because why wouldn't they want these moments, the rapture of first or early love, to continue forever, to be locked, never-changing? When you're young you can't imagine the feelings or desires you have at any precise moment will ever change, at least I couldn't when I was young, and I imagine my father couldn't either.

But he learned soon enough. *Don't ever marry for sex,* he once advised me, *it wears off in six months.* He was thirty-five when he told me this, married for fifteen years to my mother. I don't remember ever seeing him and my mother kiss or hug each other, though they stayed together for thirty years, a time during which I mostly remember my mother being sad or angry.

Why is it so hard to keep to that melody we once heard so clearly, those rhapsodic moments of early love and desire?

The last two lines of the "Begin the Beguine" most of us know are "*And we suddenly know what heaven we're in, /When they begin the beguine,*" but in the first version Porter wrote, the penultimate line read "*And we suddenly know the sweetness of sin.*" I wonder if my father, who had affairs while remaining married to my mother, was searching for that sweetness of sin. I spent many years searching for it myself. His one piece of advice to me might thus be translated as *keep sinning.*

Porter claimed to have written "Begin the Beguine" while he was living in Paris. He says that a friend suggested he see the "Black Martiniquois," many of whom lived in Paris, dance their native dance called The Beguine.

"This I did quickly," he wrote, "and I was very much taken by the rhythm of the dance . . . practically that of the already popular rumba but much faster. The moment I saw it I thought of BEGIN THE BEGUINE as a good title for a song and put it away in a notebook, adding a memorandum as to its rhythm and tempo."[5] Ten years later he wrote the song.

The lyrics he finally wrote are almost relentlessly rhapsodic until the fourth stanza, where clouds enter to interrupt the joys of early love the song seems to be celebrating. Then comes the surprisingly dark fifth stanza:

> *so don't let them begin the beguine*
> *let the love that was once a fire*
> *remain an ember*
> *let it sleep like the dead desire I only remember*
> *when they begin the beguine*

Inexplicably, the next stanza reverses itself, pleading, even though we know it will end badly, to begin anyway: *oh yes let them begin the beguine, let them play/ Till the stars that were there before return above you, /Till you whisper to me once more, "Darling, I love you!"* It's as if the songwriter wants us to hold both desires in mind at once: to both play and not play, to dance and not dance, to be, for the space of the song, in a world where you don't have to choose, rather, you can have both worlds, one in which you can say both *yes* and *no.*

Although hundreds of versions of the song exist, it was the Artie Shaw instrumental version to which my father was drawn. Ironically, though this was the version that was the most successful, and in some ways made Shaw's career, Shaw, who was reportedly a difficult man (he married eight times), came to loathe the song because of the endless requests to play it. He would tell a journalist for *The New York Times*, "I thought that because I was Artie Shaw I could do what I wanted, but all they wanted was 'Begin the Beguine.'"[6] Disgusted with the music business, he would put down his clarinet at age 44 and never pick it up again.

My mother told me once that Shaw's "Begin the Beguine" had been "their song" when they first met. "Your father was such a good

---

[5] William McBrien, *Cole Porter* (Vintage, 2000), p. 188.

[6] Prial, Frank J. "At Home with: Artie Shaw; Literary Life, After Ending the Beguine," *The New York Times*, August 18, 1994.

dancer," she added, which is perhaps the nicest thing I ever heard her say about him.

~

Is it wrong to remember the good about people instead of the bad? Or the bad instead of the good? I've always hated it when people refuse to acknowledge what is dark and destructive in others, or in a culture. How can we learn to avoid that dark if we don't acknowledge it exists? How can we say we know a person, or a culture if we avoid talking about their shadow side? How to balance the destructive part with what was good?

I wonder what I've gained by holding onto the image of my father as a fatal alcoholic, choosing to privilege that image of him over all others these last twenty-eight years. Remembering him like that didn't protect me, or my son from falling into the same river.

If I hold in mind other images, images of him dancing, playing the piano, if I remember his simple love of "Begin the Beguine," what horrifying thing might happen? Might I tumble into some pit of nostalgia from which I would never recover? Would it be falsifying who he was to privilege, sometimes, his better moments? Might it comfort me to remember a fine-dancing, musically-inclined father? Maybe I need to try harder to remain in that final tension the lyrics ask of us near the end of the song he loved, that *Yes* and *No*.

My walk's over. I'm almost to my small hotel in the Marais, where I'll soon enter the claustrophobically tiny elevator to my claustrophobically tiny room on the fifth floor. I resolve not to be claustrophobic in my memories of my father.

I resolve to sometimes remember him dancing without the darkness, to remember him pulling my mother close then opening the embrace, his hips swerving to that almost rumba beat, the clarinet sweet and high as an angel's voice, Ella crooning, promising *what moments divine, what rapture serene.*

I promise not to forget, though, how it all ends.

III

Parking Lot Nights

In the end, the most important thing I want to say is what we are playing is not merely a game... In this world we find a feeling of existence we cannot find in the real world. This does not mean we are escaping, nor that we can only play games.... Do not think playing games is a waste of time, because the game made up for something we lost.
—Anonymous *World of Warcraft* player

When my ex-husband calls to tell me our son has died—what he actually says is "It's Gray, he's gone"—I'm playing a video game Gray introduced me to several years earlier, *World of Warcraft* (*WoW*). In the game, my main avatar is a night elf healer whose most important role is to keep a group of players alive in fights against powerful foes that occur in instances called dungeons and raids. I don't remember what I'm doing when Gray's dad calls. Maybe I'm rambling about Draenor, a land filled with exotic beasts, lush forests, and rivers full of fish, looking for a new quest, or, farming elite bulls to build up a supply of savage blood, a material needed to craft superior armor. It's likely, though, that I'm in a dungeon when he calls, and that I abandoned the group during a battle. Maybe the group members all died, although in the game, unlike in real life, players can resurrect their avatars after a short time. As a druid healer, I even have a special spell to immediately bring a player back to life.

"He's gone," Gray's dad says again. His voice cracks. He won't say the word, won't say he's *dead*, but something rips in me, and I choke out a sound. My husband will say later it sounded like something between a wail and a howl, some sound that only comes out of us when our world is split open.

The last time Gray had visited, a few months earlier, we'd played *WoW* together, touring the new landscapes that had come out since the last expansion, and fighting together in a dungeon. He'd created a new toon, a hunter he called Wintermuter, after the AI character in *Neuromancer*, the cyberpunk novel by William Gibson. I'd invited him to join Mything Persons, the *WoW* guild I was a member of, and he'd stayed up late a few nights while I slept, leveling his character and chatting with some of the older members of the guild whose avatar's names are Bylbo and Awe.

"Awe walked me through some stuff for like two hours answering questions," he told me one morning during the visit. "Very nice people in this guild."

"That's why I like it so much," I said.

"Yeah, he made a big point of explaining that we were a 'fun' guild, and pride ourselves on having manners."

Though I respected Awe, Bylbo was one of my favorite guild members. I'd never met him in person, but I'd interacted with him for about five years in the guild in various ways. He'd run me through some difficult instances so that I could level up faster, spending time that benefitted only my character, and did nothing for his. And once, when Nightshalais, my healer avatar at the time, hit level 80, he gave me some rare armor that his toon, who was a leatherworker, had made.

"Not taking no for an answer," he texted through guild chat. "Someone did this for me when I hit 80, and now I'm doing it for you."

Gray and I shared a love of science fiction, fantasy and video games, and when I had the task, the day after his father called, of writing his obituary, the second thing I highlighted, after acknowledging his work as a musician, was his love of video games, indeed of all things digital. The games he played illuminated some parts of his life I might otherwise never have known. Among the most intimate communications we had as mother and son were often via the digital world: gaming, texting, and sharing music and photos through social media. Without that connection, our relationship would have been impoverished, since for at least a third of his life we lived hundreds of miles away from each other, sometimes over a thousand. My job as an English professor limited where I could live, and Gray chose to stay in Texas once he became an adult, near where his father lived.

Gray was born in 1984. Many of his generation have spent a significant amount of time in the virtual worlds of gaming. In a world of global warming, terrorism, increasing racial tensions, skyrocketing opioid deaths, a world that sometimes seems to lack moral leadership, it might make sense to sometimes want to leave this world for another where you feel that you have agency.

At the service we hosted a few days after Gray's death, we played a music video from Ghosthustler, a North Texas band he'd been a founding member of. The video had gone viral when it was released. *Spin* magazine would recommend it as one of the year's "must see" videos in 2007. One reviewer wrote that Ghosthustler had taken "gaming geekdom to a whole new world with their throwback Nintendo-chic electro rave-up."[7]

The video features a Ghosthustler song called "Parking Lot Nights," and begins with a shot of an old TV from the '80s or early '90s, a Nintendo console sitting atop it, a controller hanging down, as if someone has just stopped playing a game. At first there's only static on the TV, then as the music starts—a synthesized bass—we see close-up shots of hipsters being punched by someone wearing a Nintendo Power Glove. The video then cuts to a shot of someone driving around an urban landscape at night wearing the Glove, which is clapping the steering wheel to the synth beats of the song. The two band members, Alan Palomo and Gray, appear inside the television set, Alan singing, Gray playing a keytar. Alan's out front, and is clearly more at ease with his role than Gray, who stays in the background, mostly looking down at the keytar. Near the end of the song Alan grins and flashes charismatic smiles, while Gray breaks one small, tentative grin. He rubs his beard, as if he's not sure what they just did was worthy, or sucked big time. I will learn from a friend of his, years later, that he had just come from a period of using heroin and "kicking it," according to the friend, who added, "it wasn't pretty."

---

[7] Cam Lindsay, "Ghosthustler Parking Lot Nights," Nov 12, 2007 http://exclaim.ca/music/article/ghost-hustler-parking_lot_nights

When I first saw the video, it was after a period when Gray, not yet twenty, had been angry with me for having him committed for chronic substance abuse. He hadn't spoken to me for a while after he completed the court-required AA/NA meetings. He'd taken off to live in California with some friends for a time before returning to Dallas. When he sent me the video, it was the first contact in almost a year. He struggled with depression all his life—part of the diagnosis when he was committed was bipolar disorder—and a smile from him was a rare thing. I watched the video over and over just for the smile.

I'm not a music critic, and as the mother of one of the band members, can't objectively describe Ghosthustler's music, but critics have alternatively described it as retro-electric disco pop, barebones electro punk, disco synthesizer pop, and blog house music. You can listen to it here and decide for yourself.[8]

At some point the video shows the car being driven into a parking lot where a break-dancer does his thing on top of a Nintendo Power Pad mat, after which he, too, gets punched. The video cuts back repeatedly to the band, the TV and the Nintendo console. More people are punched and zapped by the Glove, which waves them to come forward before the zapping occurs. They illuminate and are vaporized much like antagonists you might kill in a video game.

Pete Ohs, the video's director, said he wanted the video to suggest going back to a simpler time when kids would hang out at the parking lot for fun. Playing video games, he seems to suggest, offers that same pure fun. When Alan sings at the opening "when your mind aches and your body shakes . . . I think I need to take a break, because there's only so much I can physically take," it's hard to imagine it's not the real world that's the cause of this need for escape.

At some point near the end, Alan starts clapping along with the beat, and the person operating the Glove claps too—one hand gloved, one ungloved, evoking collaboration of the gaming world and the real world.

The video highlights one way in which game dynamics offer potent metaphors by which some of us have come to engage reality. The

[8] "Parking Lot Nights," Ghosthustler, Alan Palomo and Gray Gideon, 2007. Music video directed by Pete Ohs. https://www.youtube.com/watch?v=XvaH6s8LckU

image of the car being driven with the Nintendo Glove suggests gaming as a form of travel. In the same way that those with respiratory ailments used to be advised to travel abroad or somewhere with weather more amenable to their cure, so does "Parking Lot Nights" suggest the "travel" of video games as a kind of healing.

I will come, eventually, to learn first-hand the healing role that some video games can play.

Mihaly Csikszentmihalyi's famous definition of flow as "the satisfying, exhilarating feeling of creative accomplishment and heightened functioning" describes precisely the feeling gamers have while playing a challenging game. "Games," he wrote, "are an obvious source of flow, and play is the flow experience *par excellence.*" Csikszentmihalyi would write that "alienated children in the suburbs and housewives in the homes *need* to experience flow. If they cannot get it, they will find substitutes in the form of escape." [9]

The night of Gray's service, his friends hosted an event that featured a room where those interested could play classic games like *Mario Brothers* and *Pacman* on a big screen. As I watched this mourning tribe operate joy sticks and use game controllers to navigate mazes and engage in fights on the screen, it was clear that playing these games was more than an escape for them. Instead, it was a way of remembering and connecting with a lost friend. They were engaging in an activity as sacred and genuine as those rites a community might enact in a church.

Another example of how the playing of video games can encourage an almost tribal connection between those who otherwise don't know each other well happened when I came into my stepson Rob's life. He was fourteen, and it was difficult to develop a relationship with him at first until I learned that he also played *WoW.* Once or twice I watched him play, and learned something about him that I had not had the opportunity to see in real life. He was friendly, generous even, in the game. In a complex set of monster-infested tunnels where the goal was to find a few well-hidden treasures, he put his own character at risk to stay and help another player locate the treasure Rob's avatar had already found. I had not yet had the

---

[9] *Beyond Boredom and Anxiety*, pp. 36, 37. Also see *Reality is Broken: Why Games Make Us Better and How They Can Change the World*, by Jane McGonigal for a deeper discussion of the relationship between video game play and flow.

opportunity, in real life to see this compassionate side of Rob. Since then, throughout the thirteen years I've been with his father, when I was unable to engage Rob in conversation about the real world, we could almost always exchange a few words about *WoW*. His name is right under Gray's in my friend's list.

A few days after Gray died, Rob texted me: "I remember the moment that I first met Gray. Though he was older, and I did not know what to do at first, it took us all of five seconds to bond over something as tedious as *StarCraft*. His thoughts were right along the same page as mine for the future of the franchise. It may seem trivial, but the chance to connect with someone new who somehow/someway shared my thoughts was an unexpected delight."

When Gray was much younger I initially tried to keep him away from computer and video games. I feared, as many parents do, that they might encourage violence and become addictive, contributing to isolation for one who already suffered social anxiety. But his father didn't share my fears, and as we'd divorced when Gray was very young, and shared custody, games became part of Gray's life. Eventually his father remarried and had another son. Gray and Michael grew up playing video games, often together. I would stay single for most of Gray's life, not remarrying until six years before his death, and never having any other children.

I never purchased a Nintendo, Playstation, or Xbox when Gray was young, but at some point, the gaming consoles from his father's house migrated to our house. It happened when Gray was in third grade. He'd come home from school complaining that his feet hurt. I had him take off his shoes and socks. On the bottom of both feet were large warts, Plantar warts, as I would later learn. They were contagious, the podiatrist said, and would have to be cut out. Gray, who was an active kid who'd already been diagnosed with Attention Deficit Disorder, would have to be kept off his feet for two weeks after the surgery, he said.

"And just how am I going to accomplish that?" I asked.

The doctor didn't hesitate: "Video games."

And so it happened that I caved on the video game issue. His surgery went fine, and the video games helped keep him occupied while he was unable to walk. Though I didn't play them, I watched him play, and remember those first games and their seductive worlds: *Final Fantasy*, *The Legend of Zelda*, *Secret of Mana*. Gray was good at them, and I noted he had no attention problems when playing video games. He was especially proficient in strategizing how to kill monsters or bosses. It was revealing to see how cunning he could be using some special skill or weapon his character possessed.

Over the next few years those games provided safe spaces where he could join a group of characters, sometimes virtual, sometimes real, that had the role of rebelling against and conquering some powerful evil that had taken over the world. Sometimes, as in *Secret of Mana*, the characters began as young boys who enact what is surely a version of every child's fantasy: They disobey their Elder's instruction, trespassing into a waterfall where there's a treasure. Gray learned how to be successful in these games, unlike his relentless struggles at school where he was always being sent to the principal's office for some infraction or another.

One particularly difficult teacher-parent conference from his time in third grade went like this:

"He doesn't seem to be writing down the homework assignments," Ms. Pollan, his teacher said. "Sometimes he doesn't do the work in class, either, or turns it in half-done. I'm also having behavior problems with him. Sometimes he speaks out of turn. Often, he doesn't appear to be paying attention. Sometimes he draws action figures instead of doing math." At this point she pulled out some well-drawn sketches of Ninja Turtles. She handed them to me, shaking her head.

"I see," I said, miserably.

"Sometimes he reads books in class that are not assignments. Sometimes he drums his pencil on his desk and annoys both me and the class. And he won't stop, although I ask him over and over!"

I cleared my throat. "Yes, well, his father used to do that as a child. And I sometimes have that problem with him too."

He often came to class late, she said. He was always forgetting something. He was disorganized, papers were always falling out of his desk. Sometimes he forgot his textbooks. *Sometimes*, and she caught my eye in a meaningful glance at this point, he argued with her about something she was trying to teach the class, and *sometimes* he even tried to correct her. He even argued with the authors of their textbooks, she said.

And so it went, on and on. I put up with the litany of complaints because I figured she was going to end with something positive—she just had to get the bad stuff out of the way first.

"Maybe we should up his dose of Ritalin," she said. Gray had been on Ritalin for ADD for about three years at this point. I was silent. I already hated the idea of drugging a child and had no intention of "upping" the dose.

Finally, she seemed to be coming to the end.

"Do you know what else he sometimes does in class?"

I said *no*, still hopeful that she would say how he always blurted out the right answers, how he was right to criticize the textbook authors, how he was such a good reader, how smart he was for his age. I had been proud of the book report he'd written on "The Tin Soldier," his final assessment of the story being that even if you were disabled you could be a hero. In my mind, he had progressed from mere summary to literary criticism in that report. I hoped she would at least remark on how good his book report had been.

Ms. Pollan got up from her chair. "Sometimes he does this," she said, and ran, in her high heels, across to one side of the room and back again. "He will just get up and run like that!" she said, sitting down, slightly out of breath.

"What about the book report?" I mumbled, determined not to leave without at least one positive comment.

"The what?"

"The book report, you know, the one he wrote on 'The Tin Soldier'"?

"Oh, that," she closed her record book indicating the end of our visit. "It was too long. I was trying to teach them about summary."

Almost every parent-teacher conference I had in elementary school was some version of this one. One teacher told me she loved teaching, but that Gray's behavior had made her feel like she should leave the profession. Therapists diagnosed oppositional defiant disorder. Later, as Gray aged and became more defiant and even, at times, abusive, towards me, I would think back to these parent-teacher conferences and the frustration of the teachers. I considered the principal who had paddled him in kindergarten and wondered whether that experience had contributed to turning him against authority of any kind. Some of the "bosses" in the games Gray played as a boy were fat little men that put me in mind of that principal; had he ever thought of him while he was slaying the principal-look-alike bosses?

In those early days, I didn't appreciate the value of the pure play element in the games, their autotelic nature. I'd spent my life as an educator, and wanted there to be something else, something *other* than play. Something educational, *useful*. Because Gray was constantly having to make decisions in the games, I told myself they were teaching him problem-solving skills, as well as fine motor skills. I knew of studies that suggested even first-person-shooter games could contribute to building a more capable person, improving visual attention as well as the brain's ability to spread attention over a wide range of events.

Although Gray mostly played games either with friends or alone, sometimes we played together, especially games that could be played on a computer: Puzzle games like *Myst*, evolutionary games like *Darwin's Dilemma*, role-playing games like *Baldur's Gate*. It was a way of bonding, not unlike the way my family had bonded when I was a girl by playing Monopoly, Twister, Life, and card games like Hearts (none of which Gray was interested in). Later, he played games with girlfriends as well. His girlfriend Lani would tell me that they played *Diablo 3* together the entire time they dated.

During junior high and into high school Gray's bedroom, when he lived with me, was in the basement. I'd put bunk beds, a TV, VCR, CD player and a bookcase full of his books in one of the nearly finished basement rooms. We'd strung up blue Christmas lights all along the four walls. He'd set up his computer, video game consoles, amps and guitars, as he'd developed an interest in playing music. Over the summers, he and his friends would use it as a practice and play room. Sometimes one or two boys would spend the night. They'd bring instruments, video games, computers and CDs, and would stay up all night making music, talking, and playing games. At some point in the early hours of the morning they'd raid the freezer for pizza. I'd come down later in the morning to find empty pizza boxes, the smoke alarm detector disabled, and boys spread out over the floor downstairs. Sometimes they'd sleep until two or three the next afternoon. They didn't seem to care about pillows or blankets or pajamas. They fell asleep wherever they were, wearing whatever they had on, game controllers and electrical cords connecting them like spider webs.

Though as a young boy and teenager he was always more enthusiastic about the games than I, and was always reluctant to stop when it was time for bed, in the end it seemed a harmless enough pursuit, and one that allowed him to develop closer friendships with kids his age who also enjoyed games.

Gray would tell me later that when he was young he and his friends learned how to hack parental controls so that they could play longer. His creative exploration in general with computers amazed me. He was always trying to digitally break into things, steal things, or make a video game do something it wasn't built to do. In his brilliant essay "Essay as Hack," Ander Monson writes that "hacking is at heart a creative activity. It is first, simply, an exploration, an opening up, of a system .... Most hackers who illegally access computer (or other) systems do it not to break the law but because we want access. Because we see a system and we are not allowed inside it. Because we see that apparently impenetrable tower and we want to know what rests within its walls." [10]

I can't imagine a better way to think about how Gray often engaged the world, both the digital world as well as the real world. Whether it was running up a slide in a playground instead of sliding down it, doing the very thing a teacher asked him not to do, or hacking into systems so that he could procure some game or video or movie without paying for it, he rarely respected walls that had been put up to curb that exploration or pillaging.

In late spring of 1999 I became ill, and developed sensory-neural hearing loss because of the illness, which rendered me deaf in one ear. I started on a nine-month treatment that involved daily injections and caused flu-like symptoms. Gray had just turned fifteen in May. Knowing how much he loved computer games, I'd searched to find one for a birthday gift that I could also stomach. Once again, I wanted one that had some educational value but was still fun. There had to be some killing and destruction for

[10] Ander Monson, http://otherelectricities.com/swarm/essayashack.html

him to want to play it, but there also had to be some redeeming social value in it for me to purchase it.

Up until then, we'd always gone camping during the summer. The tent changed shape and color every few years or so, the landscapes varied, but every summer we'd be outside. Every year he learned a new outdoor skill and got a new privilege. Once it was a Swiss Army knife, which he used to whittle branches on which we toasted marshmallows. Another year it was a fishing pole, which he used to help us catch some dinner. Yet another it was a camp axe, which he used to make kindling for the fire. We'd been all over: One year it was The Black Hills, another Yellowstone, and yet another Banff and Jasper. This year, because of my sickness, we'd be camped instead in rural Iowa, where I was now teaching, in front of the glow of the computer screen.

I hoped we could learn some new games together and share strategies as a way of bonding. There were movies we could watch, of course, and books we could read together, but I knew reading and films could not engage him fully, and I also knew, through previously failed attempts, that trying to get him to spend time outside (swimming at the local pool, for example) was fruitless, and, the last time he'd visited, had led to a huge argument. He did have a couple of friends in Iowa, children of my colleagues, who played music and lived in a nearby town. I'd set him up with guitar instruction with the musician husband of another colleague, but I knew that wouldn't be enough. We lived in a small town of 800, thirty miles north of the university where I taught. There wasn't much for a teenager to do.

I finally bought a turn-based empire-building game we could play on the Mac: *Civilization,* which had equal amounts of fighting and education. The game begins in 4000 B.C., and moves through contemporary times. As a leader of one of many civilizations, the goal is to build a successful empire and learn to manage resources. It's important, in the game, to balance diplomacy with aggression, and to collaborate with leaders of other countries. You must find the right mix of science, technology and the arts. Assembling armies with weapons and new technologies, you can declare war on other civilizations. This is the part I thought Gray would

150

like, the fighting and declaring war part, while I would enjoy exposing him to ancient civilizations and the need for balance and cooperation. Something for him, something for me.

Gray arrived that summer with his guitar, a backpack full of CDs, gaming consoles and a host of video games I knew I wouldn't be interested in playing with him. But he liked *Civilization* well enough, and we sometimes played together, took turns, or I sat next to him and watched him play, and let him teach me about strategy. I learned how to defend the cities I was building, and the values of using different kinds of troops. I learned to look at the city's environment not just in terms of its aesthetics, but its ability to be defended. A grove of trees not only provided resources for building, but protection from enemies. A river provided resources, but also some protection. It was good, for our relationship, that he had a chance to show me something instead of vice versa.

At the beginning of *Civilization,* one settler and a warrior appear on the screen amidst a small bit of land. You can't yet see the rest of the world, and must decide where to build your first city, and where to move your figures for the world to be revealed. I loved to see the figures that represented my civilization moving through the world. The poetry of those digital guys lighting the world by their movement most seduced me to continue playing *Civilization.* Li-Young Lee writes, in his long poem, "Changing Places in the Fire," that "We see by the light of who we are."[11] This game—as well as another we sometimes played called *Age of Empires*— graphically expresses that idea. If you don't move the figures, there's no world. It's *you,* your movement, your light, that reveals the world.

When a civilization clearly more powerful than mine attacked me, when it was clear I'd screwed up in some major way, I often didn't wait for the end to be played out. I quit the game and started over. That was always my favorite bit, the starting over part. The rich darkness of the unexplored world, no mistakes yet made, the figures on the screen hopeful (or so I imagined) for a noble and strong civilization.

In *WoW* as well, though the game as it currently exists hadn't been invented in 1999, the virtual world reveals itself as your character moves through it. Via the in-game map you can see that there might be land or

---

[11] *Poetry,* July/August, 2017.

water to explore in the distance, but its features are shadowy; you don't know its true nature until you travel there. As with *Civilization,* as with the real world, your movements illuminate the world.

If you've chosen to create a character whose main goal is to fight, let's say a warrior, in *WoW,* or in *Civilization,* you'll move through the game world looking for increasingly challenging fights. Every new species you encounter offers an opportunity for killing. A scout in *Civilization* has little power as a fighter, but can move fast and is good at exploring the terrain. A healer, in *WoW,* is not as strong as a warrior, and needs to be better at avoiding fights than engaging in them. She's best in a group where her real talent, healing, can shine. She moves through the world looking for opportunities to mend those who have fallen.

I can't help but wonder, as I think about these games and Lee's words, what kind of light Gray's body and spirit, and my own, cast in the real world, what caused us to move as we did, shaping the ways in which we understood our worlds.

When I lost a game, I'd try to figure out why, and then start over again. Gray would offer advice:

"Don't build your city there, Mom!" he'd say. "Can't you see that the enemies can reach you by boat really easily? Build it on top of that hill. It'll be harder for them to reach you."

As I watched Gray play more games, and played *Civilization* myself over that summer, I came to appreciate the more playful elements of gaming. Sometimes, just for the fun of it, I would declare war on another nation just to see what would happen. It didn't matter that I was deaf in one ear, a middle-aged woman and sick; it didn't matter that Gray sometimes had crippling asthma and was short, that he got in trouble in school, that he hated sports. All that mattered was how we played.

In later games, such as *WoW,* we both had opportunities to develop online friendships with fellow gamers who also didn't care what you looked like "irl."[12] What mattered was your gaming attitude, what armor and weapons, what magic artifacts and skills you had, how generous you were with other players, what level you'd fought to.

---

[12] An abbreviation, often used in texting, for "in real life."

After Gray left that summer I continued to play *Civilization* and *Age of Empires* over the years, along with a few RPG games like *Baldur's Gate*. *Civilization*, especially, I played for around seven years or so, off and on. It was a game that was, at the end of the day, about learning to construct something positive, at least the way that I tried to play it, avoiding conflict and focusing on arts and science. I liked that you could win through technology: you could be the first to the moon. I liked that you could also influence other civilizations by developing your culture. There were emotions I felt in this game as intensely as any in real life. Once, after spending weeks to build a beautiful capital city with wonders, great works, and a thriving and happy population, a rival civilization I had not taken enough time to court attacked my city with an atomic bomb and reduced it to rubble. Just a game, of course, but I had invested so much time and emotional capital building this city, that to see it wiped from the map in just a few seconds shocked me, viscerally.

As a kid, Gray didn't really like to think too much while he was playing games. He liked RPG fantasy games well enough, but also loved fast-paced hack-and-slash games that looked, from my perspective, like pure escape. It seemed like the adrenalin rush was the most important feature of game, the quickness, the drama. I suppose it's like the difference between those of us who would rather read poems or meditative essays as opposed to the kind of novels that focus more on action. In another parent-teacher conference I remember from elementary school, I had hoped the teacher would praise the fact that Gray read so much, but the teacher said, simply,

"He reads to escape."

The years I played *Civilization* were difficult ones with Gray. He continued to struggle in school. His report card from eighth grade notes that he did not work well independently, did not make good use of time, was not a good listener, did not follow directions, did not accept responsibility for his behavior, did not cooperate with adults, did not accept suggestions for improvement, did not observe the rules of student behavior and did not respect the rights of others. I wondered where he had learned this behavior, what I—or his father—might have done to contribute to it. When I spoke at length with a child therapist about the issue, he said, simply, "some kids are just hard-wired this way, Sheryl."

In high school Gray also got into a lot of trouble: truancy, smarting off to teachers, failing classes for not turning in work, and finally, setting fire to the school bathroom. This latter incident, along with the truancy, caused him to have to go to Texas juvenile court at age 14. He was ordered to do community service and attend a special school for a month.

As he moved into high school Gray began to withdraw from me. Our arguments about his behavior became more frequent and disturbingly intense. He still shared some things, but increasingly spent time in the summers in his room with the door closed, playing video games alone, reading comic books or music books, practicing guitar. It was also around this time, his early teenage years, that he started playing the hack-and-slash *Diablo* more often, a game he'd play off and on for the next seventeen years. He didn't share much with me during these years about that game, but I could sometimes hear the music from his bedroom, gloomy and macabre, as if from a horror movie.

In Michael Clune's memoir about his childhood and the influence of video games, he writes that the games he played as a kid gave him new directions in which to grow. While his parents were trying to teach him to grow *towards* people, at some point he realized that computer games were helping him grow out, away from his parents.[13] Teenage years are a time when children strike out increasingly on their own, so it makes sense that the fantasy worlds of computer games where it's your own agency that moves the game forward, where there are no authority figures to tell you where to go and what to do, would be seductive. It's a different way of hiding from parents. It certainly felt that Gray was growing away from me during those years, and his secrecy with the games made the distance more difficult to breach.

By the time he was sixteen Gray had been on Ritalin for about ten years. In addition to ADD and oppositional defiant disorder, new therapists also diagnosed depression, although it would be a few years before he would be diagnosed as bipolar. His dad and I had become increasingly estranged, as we'd come to develop vastly different ideas about how to help Gray. His dad was in the camp of "let's find the right drug," but I was agonizingly unsure about the use of drugs. His dad's solution was to take Gray to his

---

[13] Michael Clune, *Gamelife: A Memoir* (Farrar, Straus and Giroux, 2015), p. 27.

doctor, tell him that the Ritalin had "stopped working," and have Gray put on a panoply of other drugs, one after the other, each with worse side effects than the last, in a search to find the one drug, or pill, that would make Gray compliant, and make him succeed at school. The doctor tried upping the Ritalin dosage, which didn't work, then he tried Wellbutrin, which made him "crazy" according to Gray, then Prozac, which made him "mean," according to his dad. They settled for a while on Paxil, which also didn't seem to work, but didn't have the negative side effects of the others. At some point, they gave up and went back to the Ritalin, then eventually Adderall, another ADD drug, which would be the first drug I am aware that he abused.

Over the years, his dad had taken to either avoiding my phone calls or, when we spoke, putting the best face on things. Only through very specific, prolonged questioning, could I get a sense of what was going on while Gray was living with him. Our conversations became more painful, and fewer and farther between. They would often end with one or both of us shouting or hanging up on the other, and with me sobbing, although we tried to keep our disagreements hidden from Gray.

Gray dropped out of high school at sixteen, after which he was arrested on several occasions for disorderly conduct, possession of drugs, and harassment (of a former girlfriend). He lived sometimes with me, sometimes with his dad between the ages of 16 and 19. I took him to Paris and London for a few weeks one summer, but he seemed miserable most of the time, and when I put him on the plane to Dallas, he said the only thing he would remember of the trip is that he'd like to return some time with his friends.

At home, he refused to get a job, refused to keep regular hours, refused to help around the house, often hiding bottles of beer and wine in the house. He began drinking heavily. I suspected he was abusing the Adderall, and I worried he was doing heavier drugs. He was angry and abusive much of the time, sometimes telling me he hated me, and once, that he wished I'd die, although I think he was almost always under the influence of something when he said these things. At one point, drunk, he burned down the garage of our home. I went on anti-depressants and began seeing a therapist regularly. He would apologize, much later, as an adult, for "everything" he had done as a teenager.

When he was around eighteen he began hanging out with a known heroin addict who had needles taped to his guitar. After he was arrested for public drunkenness and insulting a police officer, I learned from a former girlfriend that he'd been both abusing his Adderall, and selling it. I had him committed to a local hospital for chronic substance abuse and being a danger to himself and others. He was murderously furious then about that commitment, although as an adult he admitted I was right to be concerned about his "power" drinking at the time.

Throughout all this mayhem, he still played games—as did I—but we shared little, and didn't play together because the level of alienation had grown so monstrous. I think, though, that we both took comfort, in similar ways, in fantastical digital landscapes that had come to seem familiar.

I don't want to focus here, on the black side of his personality that developed during this time, as I've written about that elsewhere, but let's just say I needed some form of play to mitigate the seemingly unending crisis of Gray's life, and the downward spiral of our relationship. In addition to ongoing therapy, I took to crocheting, because I enjoyed the calm and predictable repetition of it. I also enjoyed making puzzles, because there was always a way to solve a puzzle if you had patience, unlike the puzzle of my son. *Civilization* was a great help because once you got good at managing your civilization you could "win" repeatedly, in different ways, and it gave so much pure satisfaction. You could adjust the difficulty level so that it always remained challenging, and when you won, you had a stupendous civilization to show for it, plus you'd learned a lot about other cultures, and that kind of learning has always been fun for me. Truth be told, it was not an easy game for me, and I often lost, but the few wins kept me coming back.

As Gray grew out of his teenage years and no longer lived with me for extended periods of time, our relationship eventually improved. He matured, was able to keep a job for a few years, and seemed, for a time, more stable. Sometime in 2008, now 24 and living in Dallas, he visited me in Pittsburgh, where I'd moved for a new teaching gig. Working at a job delivering food, he was as happy as I'd ever seen him, writing music, deejaying, playing in Ghosthustler, and engaged in what seemed like a healthy relationship with a woman I had great affection for, who was studying art. At one point, we were having a free-wheeling conversation about science fiction, fantasy, and role-playing games. We'd run through a discussion about *Star Trek TNG* (my favorite) and *Deep Space 9* (his favorite); we talked about the film *Wall-e*, which we'd seen together; about *Bladerunner*, which we both loved, and *Do Android's Dream of Electric Sheep*, the Philip K. Dick novel the film was based on, and which I was trying to get him to read. We'd read *The Hobbit* and *Lord of the Rings* together, and discussed the *Lord of the Rings* film series, which I liked and he didn't. I told him I was still playing *Civilization* from time to time. He told me about games he was playing, including *StarCraft, Mass Effect* and *Diablo*. We joked about some of the dorky early games, like *Darwin's Dilemma*, that we'd played on the Mac, about his love of *Final Fantasy*, and he reminded me how much I used to like the role-playing element of *Baldur's Gate*.

"You should try *World of Warcraft*, mom," he said suddenly, fiddling with the keyboard on his laptop, "it has a huge role-playing element. It's an MMOG."

"*World of Warcraft*? Why would I be interested in a game about war craft? And what does MMOG mean?" I asked.

He fiddled some more, bringing up a website for *WoW*.

"It means Massively Multiplayer Online Game. You can have millions of people playing at the same time. There's something like ten million people right now who have a *WoW* toon. Just check it out, mom. You wouldn't believe how expansive the world is, it feels endless. It's gorgeous, breathtaking really, in terms of the graphics. And you can be a healer. It doesn't have to be all about killing."

He then went on to discuss specific technical details that related to the graphics and game play, during which time I tuned out. But I did try *WoW* while he was there, since I could play it on a Mac. I found it engaging enough to keep playing off and on through several years and several expansions.

Why was I so drawn to *WoW*? Initially, I was entranced by the role-playing fantasy element and the richness and diversity of the landscapes within the game. The world in which most of *WoW* is set is called Azeroth. It's the birthplace and home of elves, dwarves, dragons, goblins, gnomes, humans, pandarens and tauren, all races that play important roles in the game. I found myself entranced by the night elves, one of the oldest humanoid races, and their world. Night elves are one of only a very few races that can choose the druid class, which affords the ability to shapeshift into various animal forms including cat, cheetah, bear, stag, storm crow and sea lion. Night elf druids are deeply connected to the natural world. The ability of the druids to transform into various animals was appealing to me.

The night elf home world, called Teldrassil resembles a forested island, but is situated within the uppermost boughs of a World tree. Each race in Azeroth has its own music, and the music of Teldrassil is particularly seductive. An arrangement of woodwind and oohing female voices makes for a rich, mysterious sound as luring as what one might expect from siren voices. It's both calming and tranquil, while giving melodic expression to the enigmatic forests that surround the players, and which might contain danger. I've heard the night elf music hundreds of times, and it's come to feel as much like home to me as my own home. If my own mind were aching and body shaking, if I needed to "take a break," I might just retreat to the land of the night elves and their bewitching, eerily erotic music.

Teldrasill, like all the landscapes in the game, is rendered with loving care and detail. As you wander its forests you come across fauns, toads, young thistle boars, crested owls and night sabers roaming about. You'll see "wisps" as well, small balls of floating light that look something like electrified dandelion seed heads, and that carry someone's spirit. It is what your night elf avatar will look like when it is killed and travelling to find its body to resurrect. I've died so many times that I know exactly what it feels like to be a wisp floating about the land searching to find your body.

Gray would only raise an avatar through level 30 in *WoW*, then go back to playing other games that he liked, including his own favorite, *Diablo*. I stuck with it, though, raising multiple characters from different levels and races to max level. Just as *Civilization* had offered me a way to both play and learn new skills during Gray's difficult teen years, so too did *WoW* during his adult years, which were perhaps scarier, because he did not live with me at all, and I didn't know what was going on with him unless he told me.

Play, and here I'm talking mostly about playing video games, cannot save us. It won't keep you from screwing up your life or engaging in risky behavior. It won't fill the hole in your heart because of a son who is clearly suffering and rejecting you as a parent. But it offers a release, a tiny refuge. In some ways, the games I played were like a form of virtual tourism. As a single mother, I could not afford to take exotic vacations every year, but escaping into the fantasy world of a game often served the same purpose as a "real" trip.

As for Gray, when I look back at his tragic, short life, I'm not sure what role video games played in that tragedy. I don't believe he was addicted to them, as he would be to substances, but he was a huge fan. There *is*, however, some overlap between the effects of some drugs and the effects of playing video games at an intense level of engagement, which elevates dopamine. The rush of playing a video game intensely can be as powerful as that of intravenous drugs. Some have, rather hysterically, called video games "digital heroin" and "electronic cocaine." Others have argued against this demonization, among them game designer and author Jane McGonigal, who suggests that whether video games act as escapist venues or engage us more fully in life, depends on the way we play them.[14] Neuroscience author Maia Szalavitz writes, "If we continue to pathologize video game use by assuming that it is simply a negative activity that must be addictive because adults think it's a waste of time, we will fail to understand the difference between ordinary and problem gaming."[15]

I'm especially interested in whether substance abuse and enthusiastic video game play are connected in any meaningful way. Drug use and video game play are both forms of escape. I'm in recovery myself, having stopped both a potentially dangerous drug use in my youth as well as drinking that continued into mid-life. I find that playing games has actually made easier my decision to stay sober. It's helpful to have something purely fun to do instead of drink.

There's no evidence that extensive video game play *leads* to substance abuse or vice versa, but overlaps do exist and are worth thinking about. Two well-known writers, Tom Bissell and Michael Clune, both in recovery from drug abuse, have published extensively on both video games and drug use, although their comments don't address, specifically, overlaps

---

[14] See *Super Better: the Power of Living Gamefully* by Jane McGonigal for a more in-depth discussion of these studies, pp. 84 and 103.

[15] http://healthland.time.com/2011/11/18/brain-changes-in-video-gamers-addiction-or-just-people-having-fun/

between gaming and drug use. Bissell writes of his love of using cocaine while playing his favorite game, *Grand Theft Auto:*

> The game was faster and more beautiful while I was on cocaine, and breaking laws seemed even more seductive . . . . Video games and cocaine feed on my impulsiveness, reinforce my love of solitude and make me feel good and bad in equal measure. The crucial difference is that I believe in what video games want to give me, while the bequest of cocaine is one I loathe. I do know that video games have enriched my life. Of that I have no doubt. They have also done damage to my life. Of that I have no doubt. I let this happen, of course; I even helped the process along.[16]

I have no doubt that playing games also fed Gray's impulsiveness and his own love of solitude, and also made him feel both good and bad about himself, as did his use of drugs. Games enriched my life. I'm not sure about Gray's. I know that there were also times when I played them too much, when they became a way of avoiding issues in my life that were painful. I am certain that Gray also used the games to escape reality, and fell under the spell a game can cast where it's more important to make the next move, to get to the next level, beat the next boss, than it is to engage in your real life. Playing a video game like this can become a claustrophobic loop that deadens your real life when you enter it too often, and in this it's not unlike the way an abuse of substances can deaden your life. When I felt this happening to me, I was able to pull out. For example, I gave my husband the *Civilization* CD at one point and wiped it from my computer when I felt myself sinking into that hole, and I also deleted an early high-level avatar from *WoW*, and stopped playing the game for several months when it felt like it was taking over too much of my life.

Michael Clune has written two memoirs, *White Out: The Secret Life of Heroin*, about his heroin addiction as an adult, and *Gamelife*, a memoir about his love of playing video games as a kid. The two memoirs rarely intersect, as the drug use occurred as an adult, while the game-playing memoir focuses on his years as a young boy. He does, however, present a scene that dramatizes

---

[16] Tom Bissell, *Extra Lives*. (Vintage Books, 2010), p. 177.

the ways in which the imagery and metaphors of *Civilization* came to him during a time when he was sick from some bad dope, alternating between feeling high and throwing up. At one point, he goes to bed:

> What was there in bed? Memories of my computer game. I'd been playing a game called Civilization. In it, you try to take over the world . . . . I was playing the Germans. I had tanks, and my rivals, the Egyptians, were still using knights on horses.
>
> As I lay in bed shaking from the bad dope I imagined line after line of horses meeting my tanks. I imagined the staccato of my tanks' machine guns, then the heavy boom of the big tank guns, then the machine guns, then the dying horses, the bullets biting the knights' faces, the boom of the big tank guns....
>
> I imagined my capital, Berlin, surrounded by lush jungle. I had built the Eiffel Tower in it. It was the number one city in the world. The dope I was doing now was deep brown. It even tasted brown. I also had the number two, three, and five cities. Egypt had number four. Thebes, brown like coffee. Do they smuggle dope in coffee? My hands shook. My legs were scratched to hell. My tanks approached Thebes inexorably. The valiant, doomed Egyptian knights sallied forth. The phone rang again....
>
> Before children arrive at the stage of wanting to be firemen or soldiers, they pass through the stage of wanting to be fire trucks or tanks. Unkillable red trucks, unkillable brown tanks. I was sunk in the mud of that stage, the heavy brown treads of the dope tanks churning my memory to mud. And killing hundreds of thousands of people. The phone rang and rang and rang and rang."[17]

What's interesting about this passage is the way the imagery of the dope is conflated with the imagery in the game, and how they combine to form metaphors that shape how Clune understands his life. At this exact point in his life the dope is killing his body and spirit. He understands that dying through the lens of the doomed fighting of two civilizations in the game.

---

[17] Michael Clune, *White Out: The Secret life of Heroin*.(Hazelden, 2013) pp. 143-44.

It's almost as if the two civilizations represent two parts of his psyche that are fighting for ownership of his soul.

With respect to mixing dope and games, I can't speak for my son. I imagine his substance abuse and game-playing often overlapped, but I only know for certain of one instance, which I recount below.

In the summer of 2011, I invited Gray and his then girlfriend to spend some time in The Netherlands with my husband and me. Gray's stepdad is Dutch, and we thought Gray might enjoy meeting his Dutch relatives and tooling around Amsterdam with us. Ghosthustler had broken up, a bad break, and though Gray had retained the rights to the name, he and the new band members hadn't created music of note since the break-up. He was doing a lot of dee-jaying, and was writing some solo music using the moniker *Beige*, working on and off with another band called *Fur*. He'd lost his job, and rarely responded to my phone calls. When we did speak, he sounded depressed. When I tried to learn more about how he was doing, even questions about the new girlfriend and the work with *Fur*, he was evasive.

An actual change of scenery, I thought, might be good for him. I also wanted to get more of a sense of how he was doing by having him close for a few weeks. Having the girlfriend, who we'd never met, along, I thought, would make it more fun for him.

A few days before they arrived, he Skyped to tell me that he'd just found the girlfriend was pregnant.

"We made a mistake, mom," he said. "Neither one of us is ready to be parents." Silence. "I don't want to be a parent until, like, age 48."

I wondered silently where he had gotten the number 48, what that number meant to him.

And then, "We've decided to get an abortion."

"Are you sure that's what you want?" I asked. Having had an abortion myself, I knew how anguishing the decision could be. My heart also sunk because, selfishly, I wanted a small child in my life again, and yet I knew he was barely keeping it together himself and couldn't possibly care for a child.

He took a drag from his cigarette and pushed back a lock of his hair.

"Yeah. She's not the one, mom. I understand if you don't want to do this, but could you loan us the money for the abortion?"

He and the girlfriend, a dark-haired, tattooed petite woman, arrived in Amsterdam a few days later. We all knew about the abortion that was to happen when she returned to the States, but didn't speak of it. We were there to enjoy ourselves. To be on vacation. So, we did all the things one does on vacations, pretending everything was fine.

I learned later, from one of his friends, that when Gray and the girlfriend returned home he gave her the money to have the abortion, but sent her to the clinic alone while he did meth and played video games nonstop. He confessed this to a friend, and also that he was deeply ashamed of his behavior. I can picture him sitting in front of his computer playing, say *Diablo*, at a frenetic pace, the rush of the game doubled, tripled by the meth, the shame of sending the girlfriend off by herself to get the abortion muted, for the moment.

Gray sometimes saw his life through the lens of video game tropes. For example, he often said to me that he couldn't remember much about his childhood. He said he was thinking about naming one of his toons "Skip Intro" in honor of that childhood he couldn't remember. "Skip Intro" will be familiar to any gamer as the thing you do when you don't want to watch the video that sets up the game you're playing because you've already seen it several times.

I also think some of the tropes we find in *Diablo* give insight into his life. In preparation for writing this essay I dusted off my level 8 Diablo character and played up to level 20 to see if that playing might give me more insight into why Gray loved the game so much. As I was playing, I thought of the rich world of *WoW*, the expansive deserts of Uldum, with its archeological treasures and campy references to Indiana Jones, the vibrant underwater world of Vashj'ir with its tropical underwater life, including turtles and sea horses you can ride, and the hugely diverse world of Draenor with its thousands of quests. Nothing like this in Diablo, just the same dark tunnels over and over, the same bloated corpses and unholy creatures chasing your character, and its unending horror music. I don't wish to demonize *Diablo*, which Gamespot named as one of "The Greatest Games of All Time" in 2005, and which many game critics say is "just plain fun," but playing it again reminded me of why I hadn't liked it in the first place. It had nothing like the nature-loving druidic world that initially pulled me to *WoW*, although as I leveled in *WoW* I would often find myself in some dark places, facing what seemed like endless mobs, my character dying multiple times, floating as a dandelion seed-like wisp to find my body. But I could always choose to move to a less frantic and intensely dismal area in *WoW*. In *Diablo*, no such choice exists.

Set in the fictional Kingdom of Khanduras, the user's character in *Diablo* is usually a lone hero fighting through undead to rid the world of the Lord of Terror, known as Diablo. Beneath the town of Tristram, which lacks the charm of most of the towns in *WoW*, the character journeys through seemingly endless dungeon levels, which include crypts, caves, and winding catacombs, ultimately entering Hell itself. It's a much more conscripted space than that of *WoW*: there's only one town where you can gather supplies, rest and talk without the threat of undead or other unholy monsters attacking, and the quests are usually doled out one or two at a time (in *WoW* you can have 25 quests at a time). The dungeons are also predictable, and limited in terms of where you can go. There's almost nowhere you can't go in *WoW*, although entering certain areas will get you killed if your character is not a high enough level.

It's a much shallower game, but as one player wrote "it's a rich gameplay experience nonetheless, and it's the distilled essence of kill-things-and-take-their-stuff."[18] Some would say it's ridiculous to even compare the two games, that it's like comparing apples to oranges: *WoW* is an open world MMORPG, whereas *Diablo* is a hack-and-slash game.

Gray told me, when he was a child, that he liked enclosed places, which may suggest one reason why he was drawn to *Diablo*. But the world of *Diablo* is a dark one, and may also have better matched Gray's views of the real world, which were not sunny. Clinically depressed most of his adult life, he threatened suicide a couple of times. The journey of, in his own words, "a self-medicating drunk and addict" was nothing if not a journey towards self-destruction.

I can't help but think that those mazes, graveyards, tunnels and underground catacombs and crypts of *Diablo*, the multitudes of undead,

---

[18] Brainiac4 http://boards.straightdope.com/sdmb/showthread.php?t=651910

including succubi and demons, that chased after his character echo something about his real life and the labyrinths he created for himself through poor choices. Maybe his search for the darkest most powerful demon of all can be understood as a search for his own shadow, the final Boss.

In Ursula Le Guin's *A Wizard of Earth Sea*, a book that Gray read as a boy, a young wizard named Ged accidentally releases a powerful shadow creature that pursues him throughout the novel until he finally turns on it and chases it himself, only to find its name is the same as his own. Perhaps the search for the Devil in *Diablo* echoed, darkly, a search for that destructive part of himself.

Sometimes my own search for reasons for his tragic life and death feels like the time I spent playing *Diablo*, trying to find something of my son, going deeper into dungeon after dungeon. That search often had exactly the feel of a high-level maze filled with traps and monsters, where the entrance has disappeared and you can't find the exit. Sometimes I wonder if, at the end of the day I was searching for my own Diablo, the Mother who worries she might be responsible for the death of her son.

As someone who, in the real world, saw himself as a rebel, and rejected much of what society said was "good" (formal education, not smoking, not drinking or using drugs to excess), it also makes sense that Gray would be drawn more to the dystopian world of *Diablo*. In *This Boy's Life*, Tobias Wolff writes that there are two kinds of people in the world: citizens and outlaws. Gray would have considered himself an outlaw, indeed he once used the word "crook" to refer to himself, and perhaps *Diablo* is more suited to the outlaw mentality.

While writing this essay, which was often painful, I sometimes avoided writing by playing video games. They provide clear guidelines, clear rules, and the ability to win, unlike writing, where you are often creating the rules as you go along and you don't always know if you're successful. The downside of gaming is that it can interrupt your life, can take the place of it, or interfere with it, as gaming sometimes did with writing for me.

Instead of finishing this essay, for example, I could enter the world of Azeroth. Imagine, if you will, that it's snowing outside and I've put aside my writing. Everything is rounded and softened; the sharp lines of the stiff, tall Pittsburgh houses seem relaxed just a little. Instead of being curled up in front of a fire writing, I'm curled up in front of my computer, pillow for my back and afghan for my lap, cat at my feet, shades up so I can see the snow. I would be willing to bet that there are many others in my neighborhood curled up right now, like me in front of the light of their computers instead of those roaring fires that once kept us warm through a cold night.

The weather outside is not the same as the weather in Azeroth, where I might be questing in Stranglethorn Vale, a virtual coastal rainforest. In Stranglethorn, maybe the rain's as thick as the real snow outside. It's pouring, gray with rain, and difficult to see as I pick my way through thick brush, trying to avoid apes and panthers, tigers and pirates.

This is both the beauty and the darkness of video games. For a space of time you can separate yourself from whatever the weather is outside, or the situation. Maybe I look up from time to time to watch the snow falling and admire the beauty of it, then turn back to a hot, steaming jungle where the rain sounds just as it does in real life and where I am hyper-focused, at the moment, on a clear goal: kill x number of tigers and bring their meat to a small camp in the midst of the jungle.

This is flow. Playing the game at this level of engagement puts you in a sort of netherworld where you're mostly, but not completely, separated from the real world and its problems. I could let myself fall even more deeply into the imagined world. I could put aside for the moment the pain of my son's death, that at the end there was nothing I could do to help him. Even though I have nightmares almost every night about his life and death, I can enter Azeroth and put those nightmares aside for a few moments; I can fight monsters that I can best. I don't forget him, but I'm able to engage fully in another activity for a time that brings me some small pleasure.

Last spring, a friend of mine who is a poet and administrator of a program at a local university, and who also plays *WoW*, told me how he walked outside one recent spring morning, looked at the startling blue sky and found himself thinking it wasn't as bright as the sky in Azeroth. The graphics in the game are so stunning, so "real," it's easy to forget that the life we wake to each morning is not so stunning. It's easy to forget, too, that virtual cities in a video game are based on real cities, not vice versa. If you play the game long enough, metaphors for how you understand the world can begin to confuse themselves.

My main *WoW* character has always been a healer, but I've also created several other toons (called "alts") over the years whose role is damage, and although I'm a self-proclaimed hater of violence, I've often found myself enjoying coming home to kill things. My job as a professor and director of an MFA program means I must be reasonable and diplomatic 24/7, when sometimes I feel the opposite. Instead of lashing out at colleagues and students, I come home, climb on my treadmill with the adjustable desk in front of it, and kill monsters and bad guys, or heal allies in the virtual world. It's also a treat, for someone who works exclusively with words, to come home and play in a world that's so visual, so aesthetically stunning. I enjoy the quests that offer rewards, and which allow you to make clear progress, something that doesn't always happen "irl."

In real life, I'm an avid crocheter and knitter, so I picked up the tailoring profession for my main toon, and enjoy leveling up that profession to create more powerful armor. In real life, I collect essential oils and craft salves, lotions, massage oils and soaps with them, so I also picked up alchemy as a profession for my healer, where she collects plants and oils to make potions and elixirs that give my avatar special powers. I like to fish and cook in real life, and my avatar has max level on these professions too. She thus has some of the interests I have in real life.

Sometimes, in the years I played *WoW* I continued to experience health issues that I learned were chronic, and returning to play my now very powerful night elf healer made me feel a bit better about my aging and ailing body. Sometimes it was one of the few things, aside from therapy, journaling and writing, and a life-long working with yarn, that got me through my own episodes of chronic depression.

I seem to have a huge need for significant down time to be as productive as I am in my professional life. Games provide me with a way to be intensely idle. At the end of an hour playing a game at night I feel invigorated and challenged, as if I'd taken a brief vacation, and in a way, I have. I've gone to another world for an hour, one that didn't cost anything but a few pennies at most, and hardly any fossil fuels. I'd be ready to go back to reading and writing and teaching in the morning.

As for Gray, I think that what used to be an innocent kind of play—like that evoked in "Parking Lot Nights"—became, over time, infected by his drug use, just as most of his relationships became infected with it. Did I wish he'd have spent more time looking for a job, contributing to society, and less time playing games? Yes. But at the end of the day, the games kept him off the street and provided a place of refuge for one who suffered, as he grew into a young man, from clinical depression and violent mood swings as well as alcohol and drug abuse. Though he'd struggle to keep a job when he became an adult, it was the skills he learned playing video games, that exuberance and passion about game-playing and love of digital exploration that gave him a heads-up on how to operate systems like Ableton Live, a software music sequencer and digital audio workstation that would become important in his music composition, and which he and Alan would use in composing the music for "Parking Lot Nights."

The day after his death, an article appeared in *D Magazine* calling the death a huge loss for the North Texas music community, and singling out Gray's use of sampling as a member of Ghosthustler, and his general embrace of electronic music, which was rare in that community. Video games, in part, had provided him with some of the technical savvy that made that move into electronic music almost seamless. The computer had become his musical instrument, his preferred tool for composing.[19]

In February of 2014 Gray called to tell me he was checking himself into a rehab center. In a slurred, heavy voice, he said he'd overdosed on meth and heroin a couple days earlier. He'd thrown up blood and become psychotic, attempting to kill his best friend Bryce, the composer known as *Fur*, with whom he collaborated and who, I would later learn, was his drug supplier. I flew down to Dallas to spend some time in counseling with him, and to visit at the rehab center. He successfully completed the 30-day stint, and seemed committed to living a substance-free life. A few months later I flew him up to Pittsburgh for a visit.

He arrived at my house in July of 2014 looking healthy, if not altogether happy, with a gaming console, a myriad of different wires and connectors for the TV, and a backpack full of games he wanted to show me.

---

[19] "Dallas Musician Gray Gideon Has Died at 30," Chris Mosley, December 10, 2014 https://www.dmagazine.com/arts-entertainment/2014/12/dallas-musician-gray-gideon-has-died-at-30/

"See, mom," he said, handing me a controller for one game, "you can create your own avatar, and your choices will develop the character's personality over the course of the game."

I don't remember the name of this particular game—maybe it was *Halo*—but it became immediately clear as I created a character with his encouragement, that it was a first-person shooter game, and no matter the character I created, it had to be behind a weapon. I lost interest and suggested we play *WoW* instead, since I'd been playing off and on since he'd introduced it to me. I now had several max-level toons. He hadn't played it in several years, but he agreed, and that's when he created the Wintermuter character, a Draenei hunter. The Draenei are a race that look like goats from the bottom down, replete with long tails, but are sort of human from the top up. They're blue, and the males have tentacles on their chins. They speak with what sounds like a Russian accent, and are in exile from their home, something that may have appealed to Gray. I created a new warrior to play along with him called Kallisam, although I also showed off my level 90 healer, Nightshalais. I remember pointing out the green markings on her cheek, her long green hair, the epic armor she sported that had taken me so long to earn.

It was fun to take him around the updated virtual world to which he had initially introduced me, pointing out new modes of transportation, new races and professions, new ports with bigger ships, new ground and flying mounts, new forests and jungles with exquisitely rendered waterfalls, jewel-encrusted beasts, well-hidden caves with secret treasures, new cities and dungeons with fiendishly difficult bosses to defeat.

I knew there were more important things we could be doing. We could be talking about his struggle to find a job, about whether he was attending NA meetings, whether he was being compliant with the medications to control his depression, whether he was drinking or using. I did sneak these issues in while he was visiting, but I knew if I pushed too hard the response would be silence. When I look back at our Facebook and SMS messages over that year and the previous one, it seems as if most of them involve me trying to give him spiritual guidance, help him financially and get him to respond, usually unsuccessfully, to questions about how he was doing. It appeared, this visit, as if he was compliant, clean, and still hopeful for long-time recovery, but I sensed he needed some serious play time after the grueling rehab. I had come, through my own game-playing, to understand the value of pure play.

During this last visit, once his toon had leveled high enough, mid-twenties or so, we joined a group from our Mything Persons guild entering a low-level dungeon called Gnomeregan, populated by lepper gnomes and troggs. Gnomeregan has a multi-level, labyrinthine layout in which it's easy to get lost or fall to another floor, then struggle to find the other members of your group. Gray was unfamiliar with this dungeon, and had forgotten or chosen to ignore that in *WoW* you need to stay with your party in dungeons. He got separated from us in the labyrinth and wound up wandering around by himself.

In *Diablo*, it would have been appropriate to wander around on his own—you're almost always a lone hero in a Diablo dungeon, and in the rare case that you aren't, you usually don't need anyone to help you kill whatever monsters spawn. Unless you are at an ungodly high level, hanging out for some reason in a low-level dungeon, wandering around alone in a *WoW* dungeon is suicidal. They're built to be fought by groups of five characters of a specific level range. It's one of the crucial differences between *WoW* and *Diablo*. Once I realized he was gone, I sent Kallisam to look for him, also texting through the party chat box for him to come back to the group, warning he couldn't survive the dungeon on his own.

In a *WoW* dungeon, the names of your group members appear in the upper left corner of the screen, along with a bar showing how much health they have. I could see Wintermuter was losing life quickly. Too late, Kallisam came upon him, lying on the floor of the dungeon, dead. He'd tried to tackle a mob of leper gnomes on his own. Since I was playing my warrior toon, and couldn't heal him, I waited with him until the instance was over and he could resurrect. Even though obviously just a game, it was still disturbing to see his character lying on the floor of the dungeon, lifeless, me being unable to help. I also sensed that his behavior in the dungeon—leaving the safety of the group, rebelling against, or not bothering to fully learn the rules of the game, to his character's detriment, echoed his behavior in real life.

I could not have known that in just a few months we would be in the same position, except this time it would be real life.

One of the last photos he sent me—digitally, of course—after he returned to Dallas from his Pittsburgh visit, was a shot of his living room. He and Lani had set up two desktop computers, right next to each other. One had *World of Warcraft* loaded onto it, the other, *Diablo.*

On November 2, 2104 a little over a month before Gray died, we had the following text exchange, which would prove to be the last communication, in my memory, that we would have, although I had texted, emailed and called him that month, without response, in the months leading up to Christmas, to set up a visit:

> *Gray:* Have you played Civ V [Civilization V]? It's amazing!
>
> *Me:* No. Better than earlier ones? I just downloaded *Gone Home.* Have you heard of it? Causing a lot of controversy. Gamer gate.
>
> *Gray:* Oh yeah, I've heard that's really good. Haven't heard of a gamer gate connection so I'll have to look that up. As for civ v, it really does seem to keep the spirit of cv 2 and maintain a streamlined experience while lots of new aspects (religion for example). Very cool, though I will say I'm going to order and give civ iv a try because I have a slow computer and the diplomacy and culture options are supposedly more fleshed out.
>
> *Me:* Smiley face
>
> *Gray:* Lemme know how gone home goes I heard about it on a cool podcast a few months ago and it sounds interesting.
>
> *Me:* Ok. I also got Depression Quest. New WoW expansion coming out in a week or so.
>
> *Gray:* Depression quest?! Haha. Do you remember I showed you the feminist frequency videos that started the gamer gate thing?

The fact that the last communication I would remember having with him would be a relatively innocuous discussion of computer games and gaming culture, only highlights the degree to which it was one of the few things we could reliably have a conflict-free conversation about.

Gray died of a heroin overdose a few months after that last visit, on December 9, 2014. Lani, who by this time had been living with Gray for over a year, told me that the night before he died, he played a video game, listened to a podcast and tried to get her to play *Skate 3* with him.

Even though he'd completed the thirty-day rehabilitation program earlier that year, it was not easy to stay sober. All his friends drank—one of his best friends would enter rehab not soon after Gray died—and most, if not all, used drugs, including his girlfriend, who was legally prescribed Klonopin, an antianxiety drug that was also found in his system, along with heroin, in the toxicology report. He couldn't find a job for many months, and wound up spending nights playing video games with Lani while he waited for call-backs that never came. Although he finally did get an entry-level, full-time job with Amazon, it involved lifting heavy boxes. Lani said he'd hurt his back lifting boxes and was in pain, but was still going to work. We both wondered if the heroin use was his attempt to lessen the back pain. He'd told Lani that he hated heroin, and me that he had "only smoked" it. There was a needle mark, though, in the top of his right hand when they found him, and the toxicology report was unequivocal about the cause of death.

During the seven years I played WoW, I knew Gray was battling substance abuse, but could not do much about it except talk to him when he would allow it, and try to be a stable influence in his life. He was an adult, after all, and had not lived with me for the last twelve years of his life. I helped when he asked for help, nurtured when he would let me, all the while playing a healer in dungeons of *WoW* in my spare time, upping my healing stats over the years to the highest levels possible. No one would die on my watch, I promised myself. If I couldn't heal my son, I could heal others in this game to which he'd introduced me.

As a healer, my one job is to keep everyone alive. In the game I'm a druid, able to cast a spell called Efflorescence, which creates a large blossom that looks like a circle and heals multiple players who stand inside the circle. Some newbie wounded players ignore the circle, standing outside it to fight, and sometimes wind up dying. Others, equally ignorant, will stand in virtual fire or poisonous goop that attacks their health, oblivious to how quick they are dying. If a player doesn't get out of the fire or goop posthaste, there's almost nothing a healer can do to keep them alive.

Most veteran players know how to work with a druid healer and know to avoid the fire or goop. Most of them likely died several times when they first started playing before they figured things out. A death in a dungeon or raid causes damage and inconvenience, and can sometimes mean the whole team wipes, especially if it's a tank that dies, but that's all. It's more like a virtual overdose that doesn't kill you. You come back weak and stunned, but a healer can mend you quickly.

I think about Gray a lot when I'm healing in dungeons these days. In real life, I couldn't get him to stand in the healing circle I cast when he was younger, or as he aged. I couldn't keep him out of the fire, and he didn't seem to care that whatever it was he was standing in was draining his life. I had no way of knowing if he would ever stand within anyone's protective circle. He was drawn more to exploring the world, and various substances, often alone.

A few days after Gray's death I went to the small apartment he shared with Lani. It was filled with music equipment, games, records and books. The computers were still set up as they had been in the photograph. Lani had put two stockings up, anticipating Christmas. I told her she could keep his records. I took a couple of the books I'd given him, a Steve Jobs biography and a book on the art of making records. I took two shirts and a scarf I'd crocheted for him that Lani said he still wore when it got cold. We unplugged his computer. I'd suggested to his father we give it to his half-brother. But the game controller, sitting like a silent black butterfly on the desk? That, I would take.

Although I've never used Gray's game controller, it sits next to my Mac, in view when I play *WoW*, in front of a photograph from some time ago of us from happier times. A small stone box next the photo holds the recovery chip that was on his keyring when he died, along with my own recovery chip. A tarnished silver box holds some of his ashes.

Because of the way we set up Gray's *WoW* account, each time I logged on, in the months before he died, his name showed up in my friend list above the chat box. If he was online, the game told me where he was. If he was offline, it would tell me, and indicate how long it had been since he'd last logged on. He often played very late at night and early in the morning when I was asleep, so we weren't always on at the same time, but it comforted me to know he was there somewhere, with his hunter Wintermuter, exploring the same fantastic lands as I was. And if he wasn't always on when I was, he was still there, just *offline.*

Sometimes I still play Kallisam, the warrior I created when Gray was here. Every time I see her name and enter her body again, I think of Gray, and how Kallisam was his partner in crime when he last visited.

I can never know exactly how Gray saw the real world. During his teenage years, I felt a bit like those hipsters who were being punched by the Nintendo Glove in the *Parking Lot Nights* video, drawn close, only to be punched away. I found ways to heal myself and help others. Believing in the power of writing, I started a program to teach creative writing to women in recovery, and to inmates in the county jail.

I also healed others, virtually, in dungeons and raids, repeatedly.

I didn't play *WoW* for a few weeks after Gray died. But soon I felt drawn again to be in the space I'd shared with him, and created a new beginning level druid night elf healer, which I named Wintermutte, in his honor, after his toon Wintermuter. It's now my main avatar, after two years of leveling her, a level 120 healer. My playing is now mixed with sadness, as, I imagine, the playing of his friends was the evening of his service.

I often ask myself what light did Gray's body create in the real world, what had he seen in the real world that led him to want so dearly to escape it? I know that answer for myself, but I can't know it for him, or the millions of others who choose to play games as avidly as he. Or, worse, escape into the world of drugs.

What's left, from Gray, are mostly digital echoes: his avatar on *WoW,* his Facebook page, his texts and photos. His songs and a few videos. Some non-digital: words scribbled in his rehab book: *I don't want to die.* Slivers of insights into him, slivers of uncoverings and vulnerabilities, but not the whole person. I still search for him, and the pure play evoked in the *Parking Lot Nights* video.

While I remember Gray in a myriad of ways that are not connected to the digital world—the sound of his voice, his laugh, the gray shimmer of his eyes—the metaphors from gaming give me unique access to his psyche, and the labyrinths of both our linked and separate journeys.

As I move through life without him, I like to sometimes imagine a night-elf wisp following me around, that digital ball of light that resembles a pulsating dandelion seed head, searching for a body and resurrection he will never find. His name still appears in my friend's list, saying that he's *offline.*

I play to remember. I play to forget.

IV

The Ink that Binds: Creative Writing and Addiction

What is to give light must endure burning.
—Viktor Frankl

I've taught writing in universities for over thirty years. For the last twelve of those I've directed an MFA program and paid close attention to what other MFA programs are doing. In addition to constant worry about graduates finding jobs in a bleak economic climate, I also worry that some of our programs have fallen into a kind of elitism, focusing on mentorship that over-emphasizes publication and self-promotion, and that ignores the world we live in outside of academia, where, for example, deaths from substance abuse and suicides have risen to alarming levels. I mention substance abuse and suicide because the creative arts have been shown to have a positive effect in harm reduction for addiction as well as for the kinds of depression and hopelessness that sometimes lead to suicide. Too few programs make service to the community a central tenant of students' MFA work,[20] and some devalue the use of writing for the purpose of healing or creating community. I offer this essay as a call for another way.

In 2009 writer Sarah Shotland and I co-founded Words Without Walls, a creative partnership between the Chatham MFA Program, the Allegheny County Jail, the State Correctional Institution of Pittsburgh, and Sojourner House, a residential drug and alcohol treatment facility for mothers and their children.

For the last ten years MFA students, alums and faculty have taught creative writing courses at these facilities, and nationally recognized writers, such as Jimmy Santiago Baca, Dwayne Betts, Bonnie Jo Campbell, Natalie Diaz, and Mary Karr among others, whose work addresses substance abuse or incarceration, visit and interact with our populations. The work

---

[20] Although see the list at the end of this essay of some university programs where teaching underserved populations, specifically those who are incarcerated, is a core component. There may be others; these are the ones I am aware of.

we do with these groups has not only provided a much-needed service for them, it's also engaged and invigorated our MFA students, many of whom say that teaching in jails, prisons and rehab facilities has been a transformative experience for them. Some return as alums to continue to teach, and some have started programs like Words Without Walls in their home states after graduation. Last year seventy percent of the students who applied to our program said they were interested in social justice and creative writing, specifically teaching in prisons and rehab facilities. Each year more creative writing graduate students ask to be intimately involved with communities outside of academia, and find inspiration in working with and teaching those who are incarcerated or confined to a rehab facility.

Faculty have also been deeply affected by work with these groups. Some of us have been reminded of why we started writing to begin with, and why it's so important to write poems and tell stories—outside of the pressures of publication for promotion and tenure.

Here's my own tale about teaching creative writing in a rehabilitation facility.

Anna is twenty-five when she enters SoHo, as we call Sojourner's House. She's come to us from Allegheny County Jail, and is a recovering heroin addict, drug dealer, and mother of a small boy.[21] She also has an innate talent for writing. I'm struck, first, by the amount of writing Anna does—easily three times what the other women are doing, and by the quality of the writing. I'm moved, too, by both her honesty and sense of story. I find myself looking forward to her presence, to her questions about narrative and how to structure it, and to the increasing sophistication in the craft of her essays. She's generous and insightful in her criticism and support of the other women's work, and the workshop feels a little empty when she's not there.

One day, she comes in, not her usual ebullient self. Her eyes are puffy, her face swollen. She slumps down in her seat.

"All I know how to do is strip and cop drugs," she sobs. "I have a baby now. It was a mistake, but I love him. How am I gonna get money to

---

[21] All names of inmates or residents have been changed to protect their privacy.

take care of him?" She puts her face down on the table, her bleached hair stacking around her head like so many strands of a frozen waterfall.

"Dude," Holly, a normally quiet woman, offers from across the room, "chill, you can't think about that right now, just be where you are. Worry won't help, dude. You still have four more months."

Denise, a tall, dark-haired woman sitting next to Anna, one who has written about her own journey into prostitution to support her drug habit, takes Anna's hand in hers, but says nothing. Denise will be leaving SoHo next week. She's surely as worried as Anna, but doesn't show it.

I don't have answers to Anna's question, but I say something about her maybe publishing some of her writing. I tell her there are people who would be interested in hearing about her life, how she came to be an addict, her experience giving birth in prison, and her journey to recovery.

She looks up, eyes glistening.

"Really?" She's quiet for a moment, then wipes her eyes and, after we talk a bit more, picks up her pen again.

Anna almost didn't come to SoHo. She was initially upset about the fact that to get a bed here you had to agree not to wear make-up.

"There was no way I was going anywhere without make-up," she said.

So before transferring to SoHo she slipped into the jail's infirmary and stole a needle. She then fabricated some version of India Ink (soot and shampoo, she said), which she then attempted to tattoo onto her eyelids so that she would have permanent eyeliner.

"It was painful," she said, "the most painful thing I've ever experienced."

I can't see evidence of the tattooing, so I can only guess she was unsuccessful. Her large, hazel-colored eyes are beautiful enough, I tell her. She doesn't need make-up.

"The thing is," she says, "now that I've been here for a few months, I . . ." she pauses, "I realize I don't look so bad without make-up."

Many of the women in SoHo, like Anna, have come here from jail. For some, a six-month stay is required in lieu of a jail or prison sentence. Most of them have had at least one experience where they almost died from drug or alcohol poisoning. Some have sold their bodies for substances; some have gotten beaten almost to death because of drugs or alcohol. Others have children who are not allowed to see them. Since many were addicted while pregnant, there are often problems with births. One woman, who was pregnant when she started our program, gave birth to a stillborn infant while in SoHo. She knew it would be stillborn, but chose to go through labor instead of having it cut out of her. Two days later she's back in class, writing about the birth.

At least half of these women my teaching partner, Sarah, and I have come to care deeply about will probably sink back into drug use. Last year only forty-eight percent of the women in SoHo reached the national benchmark of 90 days for successful drug and alcohol rehabilitation.

Anna's drug is heroin, and she's written moving and disturbing pieces about being brought back from death. It's painful to hear her read these stories in the workshop, well-crafted as they are. The Anna I've come to know is sober and drug-free, her eyes bright and curious. During the six months I work with her I'll never see her high or at work copping or stripping, although she's not shy about sharing the details of her past life.

We ask the women to write a personal essay about how they came to be in this exact place. The road to recovery, or, if they wish, the road to ruin. Sarah and I write along with the women each week. When we started the memoir module I had to ask myself the same question I'd asked them. How had I come to be here, teaching writing in a rehab facility?

The easy answer is that I have a soft spot for substance abusers. My mother's sister died in her thirties of an overdose; my brother at twenty-three, and my father died of cirrhosis from alcoholism at fifty-nine. My son died at thirty of a heroin overdose. Both my son and my brother spent time in jail or prison. I'm in recovery myself, sober nine years, and drug-free for three-times that, but not a week goes by that I don't think about drinking, and almost not a week that the images of needles entering my vein, drawing up blood and shooting pleasure into them, don't float into my subconscious, however briefly. I've written and published poems and essays for years about substance abuse, mine and family member's, and

I know first-hand how writing can encourage healing by giving shape to chaos. I'm certain I would not be alive without writing, and I have fifty years of journals, several books of poetry and nonfiction to prove it.[22]

Perhaps one reason I believe so strongly in programs that make use of creative writing in recovery is because I used it myself to structure and channel the turmoil of my life, and I've watched close friends do the same. To make and gift a poem, a story, an essay of something dark, feels good, especially if you're able to write toward insight or deeper questioning. To witness students do the same feels just as good.

I'm moved more than I can say by the untutored poems and stories of recovering addicts, especially poems and stories that reach for introspection. Every word matters to the addict in recovery. She has no choice but to interrogate the soul. One writer from the jail wrote of lighting up a bowl when his son was born, realizing at the moment of inhale that he was in both heaven and hell. There he found the entrance to a poem.

Anna, who spent time both in jail and at SoHo, wrote a story about being pregnant in jail, giving birth at a local hospital, her child being taken away immediately and she being led off in shackles back to the jail. She hated her child at first, she wrote, and dreamed of tossing him out the window; she even envisioned how his swaddling would balloon out as he fell, but she soon came to love the child, who is now with her in SoHo. Perhaps what draws me most to her stories and others like them, is that they feel necessary, bristling with raw honesty and power. They feel true in the deepest sense; there's always something at stake.

In a world that often seems numbingly cynical, it's deeply affecting to witness the work of one for whom every word matters so deeply. One wrong word and the story is a lie. All Anna has right now are words, and the truth of how she came to be here. And while she may not realize it, her bravery in saying her truth inspires me every day. In one class she wrote:

> The only thing, besides high school, I have ever completed has been rehab. My self-esteem was not only low while in jail, it was straight up gone until I started creative writing. I wrote my pain and struggles, and when we shared with one another, I was

---

[22] See, for example, http://howapoemhappens.blogspot.com/2016/02/sheryl-st-germain.html for a discussion about the writing of my poem "Addiction."

praised with positive feedback. It was a work-in-progress to start to believe in myself. You can tell a schizophrenic that nobody's in the corner—however, it isn't going to matter what you say to him until *he* believes nobody's in the corner.

I would look forward to creative writing like nothing else. It broke up the monotony of life behind bars and for those two hours we would feel like normal human beings again—not slaves.

During a recent public reading at a neighborhood art gallery for the SoHo women, my husband said he'd not seen me so happy in a long time, happy to hear Erica, who is now out and attending regular recovery meetings, read about her struggle to survive outside; to hear Pam, who will be out in a week read about her return to her community church; to hear Charmaine, a counselor who works at SoHo and is seven years clean, read about how she abandoned her children ten years ago and understands what the women are going through.

Sarah and I were also proud of Bebe, who, despite her fears, volunteered to read first. She'd purchased a golden tunic with psychedelic, sixties-style designs from a nearby thrift store to wear to the event. We were all rapt as she read aloud about a recent experience that almost led to an overdose. An older man she'd fallen in love with had asked if she trusted him, and when she whispered *yes,* he grabbed her arm and pushed up her sleeve:

My heart starts to race and my mouth fills with saliva and a numbing sensation I've never experienced. My head is ringing and my sight blurs. I find myself releasing the breath I didn't know I was holding, quickly inhaling again, desperate for air. He takes the needle out and presses a napkin to my arm, catching the blood. He bends a little to my level and asks, "Can you feel that?"

I look around the room. All the women are listening, intent, quiet. She continues.

I stare back at him, unable to focus or respond, filled deep with a sensation I've never felt before, that to my disbelief, keeps intensifying. It scares me a little. I've never been this high before. I turn from him and stagger back to the living room. Legs shaking, I put my arm out, reaching for the wall. I can see myself touching the wall and taking small stumbling steps, but all I feel is numbness. By the time I make it to my bedroom window, my whole body is covered in a sticky sweat. I need fresh air. I try to open the lock on the window and wince in pain. I hold my arm up to the streetlight coming through the window and see the bandage around my wrist fill with blood again.

She ends the piece with a haunting image: in her stumbling she knocks over a vase that has roses in it. She looks down at the floor to see the needle lying at her feet, rose petals scattered around it.

Can creative writing save someone in the throes of addiction? Absolutely not. Some are so damaged that almost nothing can stop them from drowning in that river. Two weeks after the reading for the SoHo women, we learn that Bebe has overdosed and died. Sarah and I and the women are still grieving as I write this, mourning the loss of a young woman who had been brave enough to write and to stand up first and share her life's story.

It's important not to enter this work with the romantic notion that you are saving people. You are, rather, engaging in a relationship with each student, a relationship that is mutually beneficial. You are not their counselor. You are not their sponsor. You are their writing coach, their writing cheerleader.

When Anna was released from SoHo we hugged, and she said she'd keep in touch. I didn't hear from her, though, and I wasn't surprised. In the days and weeks following her release I tried to focus on the other women at SoHo, but she always snuck into my thoughts. Had she found a job? How about childcare for her son? Was she staying clean? Was she writing?

A few months later, I hear she's been arrested again and is back in the county jail where we also run creative writing classes. I'm due to go there for the students' final reading of the term. I imagine she'll be at the reading, and I steel myself for seeing her locked up.

At the jail, the men are led in first and take their seats in the room. I converse with them, keeping my eye on the door for the women. A few minutes later the guards lead them in, and there's Anna, clutching a notebook, her hair having grown out darker, the lumpy orange-red jumpsuit covering her body. I almost don't recognize her, though, because she has on make-up: eyeliner, mascara, blue eye shadow. She looks different—feline, *other*. She smiles when she sees me, and runs over to give me a hug. I hug back, though the guards eye me suspiciously. I remember we aren't supposed to touch the inmates.

Her eyes are bright but sad, "I've been writing," she says, holding up the notebook and flipping through it to show me the sentences filling each page.

And then, "I relapsed," she says.

"I know," I say, bowing my head so she can't see my eyes. I open her notebook and begin to read, the inky marks swirling, my eyes burning.

I don't know what will become of Anna. But then I don't know what will become of any of the students in SoHo or those I teach in the MFA program. What I do know is that Anna is a good writer and her voice deserves to be heard. Sarah and I felt so strongly about her writing that we recently published one of her essays in an anthology we edited.[23]

A few of the writers we've worked with have won awards in the PEN Prison Writing Program. Alan is one of them. A talented young man, Alan took creative writing classes with us while in the Allegheny County Jail. We published one of his stories in our annual Words Without Walls anthology and encouraged him to submit it to the PEN contest. Soon after coming in second for the PEN contest, he was released from jail and invited to do a reading in New York City with Joyce Carol Oates. Not long afterwards he was awarded a scholarship to an MFA program in New York City. Eric has now completed his MFA, and is teaching for Words Without Walls.

In 2016, I created a new program sponsored by Words Without Walls, a twelve-week creative writing Master Class called the Maenad Fellowship designed for women who have been through a recovery program

---

[23] *Words Without Walls: Writers on Addiction, Incarceration and Violence*, ed. Sheryl St. Germain and Sarah Shotland. Trinity University Press, 2015.

and want to continue a writing process. With the help of a grant from Staunton Farm Foundation we offered the women $500 gift certificates for finishing the program, and were able provide transportation and child care. The women generated creative writing every week and participated in workshops with several local and national writers. We graduated our first group in April 2017, and several of the women have already published poems and essays, taught workshops themselves and presented their work publicly. Two have recently been admitted to MFA programs, one has just graduated from an MFA program and another with a BA. Another is working on becoming a Certified Recovery Specialist.

In his recent book on addiction, doctor and author Gabor Maté recommends writing as part of a therapy for addiction. Of his own addictive tendencies, he says "I needed to write, to express myself through written language not only so that others might hear me but so that I could hear myself . . . To do so is healing for ourselves and for others; not to do so deadens our bodies and our spirits. When I did not write, I suffocated in silence."[24]

A substantial body of research illustrates both the need and value of creative therapies in the process of recovery from addiction.[25] Writing, especially the writing of poetry and memoir, offers the opportunity to become more intimate with oneself, and provides a form of expression for feelings that cannot be easily shared. The skills of creative writing, which include the ability to craft and imagine current realities and new futures and the development of a confident, mature voice, are crucial skills for those who may be released from a prison or rehabilitation facilities into a less-than-perfect world.

A few writers outside of academia have chosen to spend a significant amount of time teaching creative writing in prisons (and about 80% of those in prisons are there for drug-related crimes), most notably Wally Lamb (York Women's Correctional Institution) and Judith Tannenbaum (San Quentin). Jimmy Santiago Baca, who learned to write poetry while in prison, still teaches regularly in prisons. Dwayne R. Betts, whose book about his years in prison, *Question of Freedom: A Memoir of Learning, Survival, and Coming of Age in Prison*, has received much praise,

---

[24] Gabor Maté, *In the Realm of Hungry Ghosts: Close Encounters with Addiction* (North Atlantic, 2010), p. 384

[25] Many of these studies are cited in Friedman, H.S., ed., *Oxford Handbook of Health Psychology*. See also James Pennebaker's work: *Expressive Writing: Words that Heal*.

186

regularly visits detention centers and inner-city schools, and talks to at-risk young people.

Many others, often unknown and unsung, without the support of a university, English department or MFA program, strike out on their own. I think of Ralph Nazareth, who, over the last eleven years, has taught in the Rising Hope program at maximum security prisons in New York, or Joseph Bathanti, who has taught writing in prisons for thirty-five years. I think of my former colleague at Iowa State, Steve Pett, who taught creative writing alongside graduate students for many years in Iowa, and was an early inspiration for me.

I know of no MFA programs outside of ours that teach regularly in rehabilitation facilities, although, paradoxically, there's great interest in contemporary literature that comes out of substance abuse. One has only to look at Mary Karr's *Lit*, Natalie Diaz's *When My Brother was an Aztec*, Ann Marlowe's *How to Stop Time: Heroin from A to Z*, David Carr's *The Night of the Gun*, Tracey Helton Mitchell's *The Big Fix: Hope After Heroin*, or Michael Clune's excellent *White Out: The Secret Life of Heroin*. Of course, there's also a long history of authors writing about drug use in literature, including such luminaries as Samuel Taylor Coleridge, Thomas De Quincy, Charles Baudelaire, Robert Louis Stevenson, Aldous Huxley, Jack Kerouac, Charles Jackson and William Burroughs, to name just a few.

Despite the current "war on drugs" it's clear that imprisonment of addicts has not worked to curtail overdose deaths. While I don't believe that creative arts therapy alone can do what our country has failed to do, I do believe the current crisis is at least partially a spiritual crisis, and that creative writing can be a crucial tool as we try to work our way through this crisis. Should MFA programs continue to focus exclusively on craft, and not consider strategies by which at least some of our thousands of graduates (3,000-4,000 MFA/PhD grads a year in 2014 according to the Associated Writing Programs (AWP)[26] could be given the opportunity to teach writing to those incarcerated or in recovery as part of their graduate programs?

Most of us do this kind of work in our "spare time." Why don't we put this kind of service at the center of more of our academic programming? I would argue that the path of continuing down the road

---

[26] See AWP's 2014-2015 Report on the Academic Job Market https://www.awpwriter.org/careers/career_advice_view/3919/awps_201415_report_on_the_academic_job_market

of elitism, with our myopic focus on publishing and self-promotion is not a sustainable one.

I could make the argument others have forcefully made that creative arts therapy reduces recidivism in prisons and jails; that it produces better effects than group therapy; that it helps with PTSD; that it decreases violent behavior; that it decreases substance abuse and produces measurable benefits to physical health. But my suggestion is much smaller, though perhaps no less important. Let's build MFA programs with more heart and generosity. Let's share our knowledge, our strategies, our creative writing tools, and yes, even our students with those who could benefit from them but may not be able to afford them. Let's think about what's best for our culture, not just our programs, and along the way we just might find our programs, our students and ourselves revitalized.

Works Cited

Betts, Dwayne. *Question of Freedom: A Memoir of Learning, Survival, and Coming of Age in Prison.* Penguin/Avery, 2009.

Carr, David. *The Night of the Gun: A Reporter Investigates the Darkest Story of His Life.* Simon and Schuster, 2009.

Clune, Michael. *White Out: The Secret Life of Heroin.* Hazelden Publishing, 2013.

Friedman, H.S., ed., *Oxford Handbook of Health Psychology.* Oxford University Press, 2014.

Lamb, Wally. *Couldn't Keep It to Myself: Wally Lamb and the Women of York Correctional Institution.* Harper Perennial, 2004.

Marlowe, Ann. *How to Stop Time, Heroin from A to Z.* Basic Books, 1999.

Maté, Gabor. *In the Realm of Hungry Ghosts: Close Encounters with Addiction.* North Atlantic Books, 2010.

Mitchell, Tracey Helton Mitchell. *The Big Fix: Hope After Heroin.* Seal Press, 2016.

Pennebaker, James and John Evans. *Expressive Writing: Words that Heal.* Idyll Arbor, 2014.

St. Germain, Sheryl and Sarah Shotland, eds. *Words Without Walls: Writers on Addiction, Violence and Incarceration.* Trinity University Press, 2015.

Tannenbaum, Judith, *Disguised as a Poem: My Years Teaching Poetry at San Quentin.* Northeastern University Press, 2000.

Programs that Promote Teaching Creative Writing in Prisons

Arizona State University Prison Education Programming
Chatham University Words Without Walls Program
Goddard College Transformative Language Arts Concentration
National Association for Poetry Therapy
National Conference on Higher Education in Prison
University of Michigan Prison Creative Arts Project
University of Wisconsin Madison Writers in Prison Project

Acknowledgements

Thanks to Chatham University for a sabbatical in 2017 that allowed me to complete this book.

A special thanks to Bushcreek Foundation for the Arts, The Hermitage Artist Retreat, The Lillian E. Smith Center, and La Muse Artists and Writer's Retreat for the gift of time and inspiring places to write.

Gratitude to those who have inspired and nurtured me in ways they may never fully know: Maggi Aebi, Laura Armesto, Darrell and Karen Bourque, Linda Devos, Kerry Eielson, Dakota Garilli, Morgan Everhart, Greg Girard, Brittany Hailer, Saris Jiles, Jessica Kinnison, Lyndsay Knecht, Alan Molitar, Melanie Pruit, Janette Schafer, Jessica Server, Sarah Shotland, Holly Spencer, Aspen Stoddard, Sarah Womack, Rixt Zuidema, and my current and former students from Chatham University, the Words Without Walls program, the brave women of Sojourner House, and the Maenad Fellows.

And, as always, epic thanks to my patient husband, Teake Zuidema.

"To Drink a Glacier" appeared as "To Drink from a Glacier" in *Cultural Vistas*, Spring 2000.

A version of the description of playing in Stranglethorn in "Parking Lot Nights" appeared as "Blizzard," *Sundog*, September 2013.

"It's Come Undone: Crocheting and Catastrophe" appeared in *Stitching Resistance: Women, Creativity, and the Fiber Arts*, ed. Marjorie Agosín. Solis Press, 2014.

"The Third Step" appeared in *Fourth Genre*, Spring 2014 and in *Creating Nonfiction: Twenty Essays and Interviews with the Writers*, ed. Jennifer Hurt and Erin Murphy. SUNY Press, 2016.

"An Essay in Search of a Poem" appeared in Vox Populi (blog edited by Michael Simms), March 2014. http://voxpopulisphere.com/2015/03/20/sheryl-st-germain-essay-in-search-of-a-poem/.

"Call of the Bagpipes" appeared in *Paragraphiti*, 2014.

"Do No Harm" appeared in *Parts Unbound: Narratives of Mental Illness and Health*. Ed. Giny Levy and Matthew Bohn. Lime Hawk Books 2015.

"Fifty Miles," appeared in *The McNeese Review*, Vol. 53, 2015-2016.

"The Ink that Bleeds: Creative Writing and Addiction," appeared in *Creative Nonfiction*, Issue 63, Spring 2017.

"Memory, Ever Green," appeared in *The Texas Review*, Spring 2018.

"The Light of Who We Are," a shortened version of "Parking Lot Lights" appeared in *Iron Horse Literary Review*, June 2018.

"Hiking in Wyoming, After a Death," appeared in *Flyway Magazine*, Summer 2019.

About Sheryl St. Germain

Originally from New Orleans, Sheryl St. Germain has published six poetry books, two collections of essays, and co-edited two anthologies. *The Small Door of Your Death*, a collection of poems about the death of her son, appeared in 2018 with Autumn House Press. She directs the MFA program in Creative Writing at Chatham University where she also teaches poetry and creative nonfiction, and is co-founder of the Words Without Walls program.

Having lost a father, brother and son to substance abuse, Sheryl has long been drawn to writing poems and prose that speak for those who are voiceless, specifically those suffering from substance abuse or those in relation to them. She has also written often about the landscape and culture of New Orleans and southwest Louisiana as well as the natural disasters that have been visited on her family and home there.

See: www.sheryl-stgermain.com for more information.

Books from Etruscan Press

Zarathustra Must Die | Dorian Alexander
The Disappearance of Seth | Kazim Ali
Drift Ice | Jennifer Atkinson
Crow Man | Tom Bailey
Coronology | Claire Bateman
Topographies | Stephen Benz
What We Ask of Flesh | Remica L. Bingham
The Greatest Jewish-American Lover in Hungarian History | Michael Blumenthal
No Hurry | Michael Blumenthal
Choir of the Wells | Bruce Bond
Cinder | Bruce Bond
The Other Sky | Bruce Bond and Aron Wiesenfeld
Peal | Bruce Bond
Poems and Their Making: A Conversation | Moderated by Philip Brady
Crave: Sojourn of a Hungry Soul | Laurie Jean Cannady
Toucans in the Arctic | Scott Coffel
Sixteen | Auguste Corteau
Wattle & daub | Brian Coughlan
Body of a Dancer | Renée E. D'Aoust
Ill Angels | Dante Di Stefano
Aard-vark to Axolotl: Pictures From my Grandfather's Dictionary | Karen Donovan
Scything Grace | Sean Thomas Dougherty
Areas of Fog | Will Dowd
Romer | Robert Eastwood
Surrendering Oz | Bonnie Friedman
Nahoonkara | Peter Grandbois
The Candle: Poems of Our 20th Century Holocausts | William Heyen
The Confessions of Doc Williams & Other Poems | William Heyen
The Football Corporations | William Heyen
A Poetics of Hiroshima | William Heyen
September 11, 2001: American Writers Respond | Edited by William Heyen
Shoah Train | William Heyen
American Anger: An Evidentiary | H. L. Hix
As Easy As Lying | H. L. Hix
As Much As, If Not More Than | H. L. Hix
Chromatic | H. L. Hix
Demonstrategy: Poetry, For and Against | H. L. Hix
First Fire, Then Birds | H. L. Hix
God Bless | H. L. Hix
I'm Here to Learn to Dream in Your Language | H. L. Hix
Incident Light | H. L. Hix
Legible Heavens | H. L. Hix

Etruscan Press Is Proud of Support Received From

Wilkes University

Youngstown State University

The Raymond John Wean Foundation

The Ohio Arts Council

The Stephen & Jeryl Oristaglio Foundation

The Nathalie & James Andrews Foundation

The National Endowment for the Arts

The Ruth H. Beecher Foundation

The Bates-Manzano Fund

The New Mexico Community Foundation

Founded in 2001 with a generous grant from the Oristaglio Foundation, Etruscan Press is a nonprofit cooperative of poets and writers working to produce and promote books that nurture the dialogue among genres, achieve a distinctive voice, and reshape the literary and cultural histories of which we are a part.

etruscan press

www.etruscanpress.org

Etruscan Press books may be ordered from

Consortium Book Sales and Distribution
800.283.3572
www.cbsd.com

Etruscan Press is a 501(c)(3) nonprofit organization.
Contributions to Etruscan Press are tax deductible
as allowed under applicable law.
For more information, a prospectus,
or to order one of our titles,
contact us at books@etruscanpress.org.